The Chitral Campaign

MAJOR TOWNSHEND.   LIEUT. GURDON. SURG.-CAPT. WHITCHURCH. LIEUT. HARLEY
SIR GEORGE ROBERTSON.   CAPTAIN CAMPBELL.

OFFICERS OF THE GARRISON OF CHITRAL FORT

The Chitral Campaign

An Account of the Anglo-Tribal Conflict, North West Frontier, 1895

H. C. Thomson

LEONAUR

The Chitral Campaign
An Account of the Anglo-Tribal Conflict, North West Frontier, 1895
by H. C. Thomson

First published under the title
The Chitral Campaign

Leonaur is an imprint of Oakpast Ltd

ISBN: 978-0-85706-731-9 (hardcover)
ISBN: 978-0-85706-732-6 (softcover)

http://www.leonaur.com

Publisher's Notes

Contents

Preface

How this book comes to be written requires a word of explanation.

At the beginning of the year I had to go to India on business, and on my arrival in Bombay on March 15th, I found that a force was to be sent through Swat and Bajour to relieve the beleaguered garrison of Chitral.

Some years before I had spent a few months in Peshawur, and had become greatly interested in the Pathans, and in the wild free border life. Moreover the Buddhistic remains, found all over the Peshawur Valley and on the surrounding hills, are in themselves a fascinating study. By a fortunate chance I was enabled to visit Ranighat, a ruined city a few miles across the border in the country of the Khuda Kheyls, which is believed to be the ancient Aornos, and to bring back one or two very curious Graeco-Buddhistic fragments. Swat, the ancient Udyana, is believed to be even richer in Alexandrine remains, and I often looked longingly at the low line of hills that shuts it off from Mardan. But Swat, until this recent expedition, was a closed country. It is true that McNair and Bellew, carrying their lives in their hands, had penetrated into portions of it in disguise; but they had only been able to pass through hurriedly, and it was still practically an unknown land.

The *akhoond*, or priest-ruler of Swat, who died quite recently, (as at time of first publication), was a man revered by all the frontier tribes for his holiness and piety; and the religious fervour of the people, and their hatred of the unbeliever was so intense, that it was not safe for any European to set foot within their border. In addition to their fanaticism, they had too an ardent love for their country, and a jealous dread of aggression, or of the least freedom of intercourse that might in time lead to aggression; and sheltered on all sides by rugged mountain ranges, broken only at rare intervals by steep and difficult passes, they had for centuries been able to successfully repel invasion, and to maintain their rigid seclusion intact. It was their proud boast that their "*purdah*," or curtain, had never been lifted.

I therefore gladly availed myself of the opportunity of seeing the country in the fullest possible way by going with the force as a Press correspondent. What I have written is merely a brief narrative of the events of the siege, and of the march of the two relieving forces. I have only referred to the vexed political and strategical questions involved, sufficiently to make an intelligible narrative, and I have not attempted any appreciation of the campaign from a military standpoint. I have merely given the story and not the history of it.

In one or two places I have quoted a characteristic Afghan proverb. They are taken from the very interesting collection published some years ago by Mr. Thorburn, of the Indian Civil Service.

For the photographs of Swat, Jandol, and Dir I am indebted to the kindness of Mr. F. E. Dempster, of the Indian Telegraph Department, who has had charge of the telegraph arrangements of the Chitral Relief Force, and who has taken the line right up to Chitral itself. Those of Chitral, Mastuj, and Yasin were kindly given me by Lieutenant Beynon, D.S.O., of the 4th Gurkha Rifles, who is on special duty with the Kashmir Imperial Service troops, and who acted as staff officer to Colonel Kelly during his march from Gilgit to Chitral.

I have also to thank Mrs. Montgomery Hunter for the very vivid and accurate water-colours of the Balti and Kashmir *Coolies*, taken by her from life some years ago in Kashmir.

H. C. T.

CHAPTER 1

Assassination of Nizam-ul-Mulk

On August 30th, 1892, Aman-ul-Mulk, the *mehtar* of Chitral, died. The Chitralis always speak of him as the *"Lott"* or Great *Mehtar*, for he acquired Yasin and Mastuj by conquest, and by a series of judicious marriages raised Chitral to a position of much importance amongst the surrounding tribes. But though admirably suited to govern a savage people, he was exceedingly cruel, treacherous and vindictive; in fact, what Sir Lepel Griffin has called him—a truculent old savage. At his accession he killed all his near relations, except his brother Sher Afzul, our recent opponent, who made his escape into Badakshan, and afterwards to Cabul, where he lived in exile for over thirty years. Aman-ul-Mulk pretended to be friendly to the English, but was at first secretly hostile to them, and there is little doubt that Mr, Hayward was murdered in Yasin in 1870 by his express instructions.

The Chitralis, however, who are an Aryan race and not Pathans have a deep-rooted hatred and dread of the Afghans; and in 1878 Aman-ul-Mulk, being afraid of aggression by the Amir of Afghanistan, placed Chitral under the nominal suzerainty of the *Maharajah* of Kashmir, whose province of Gilgit borders upon Yasin. Kashmir being one of the tributary states of the Indian Empire, this brought him into direct touch with the Government of India, with whom from that time until his death he did all he could to maintain friendly relations. In 1885 a mission under Sir William Lockhart visited Chitral, and was very cordially received, and so too was Colonel Durand, who went there in 1888.

Aman-ul-Mulk was a shrewd man, and not only saw that it was desirable to be on good terms with so powerful a neighbour, but he managed also to extract a considerable amount of profit out of the connection, and was for many years in receipt of a subsidy both

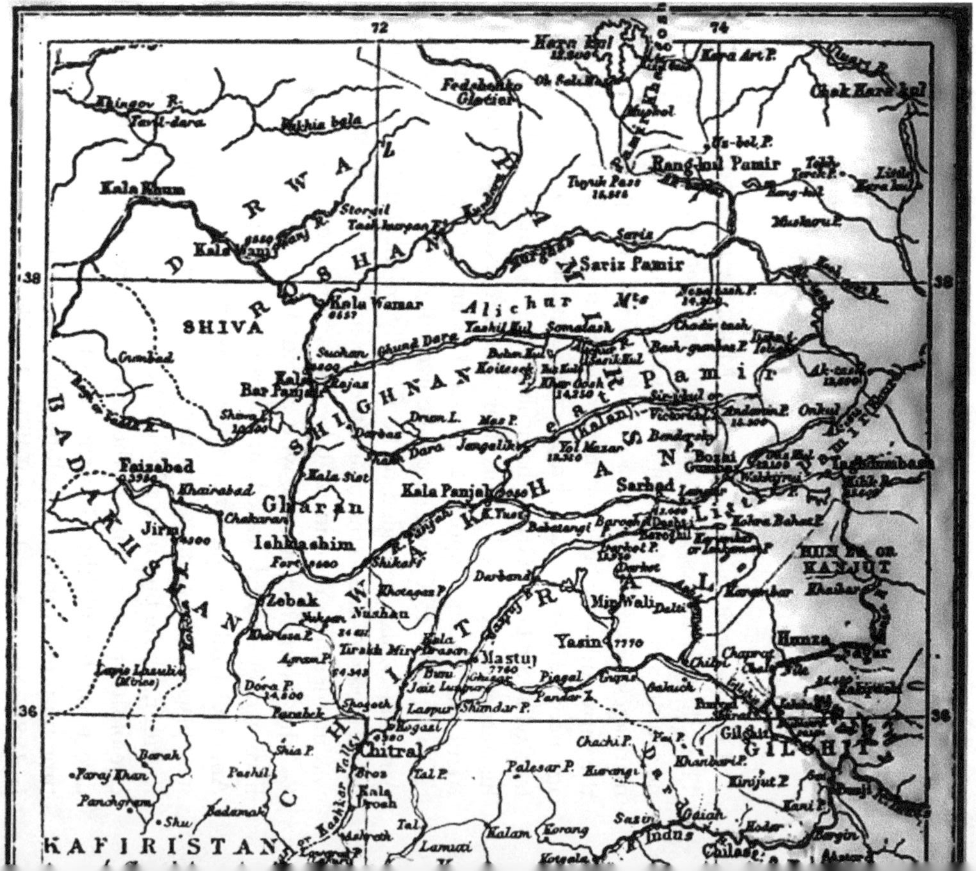
72
74
38
36
Kara Kul
Kara Art P.
Chak Kara-kul
Fedchenko Glacier
Kala Khum
Rang-kul Pamir
Tagurk Pass
D A R W A Z
Sariz Pamir
SHIVA
Kala Wamar
Alichur Mts
Yashil Kul
Somatash
Bash-gumbaz P.
Chadir-tash
Suchan
Ghund Dara
Kala Bar Panja
Rajas
Koitesek
Khar Gosh
P a m i r
Drum L.
Mas P.
Darbas
Jangalik
Yol Mazar
Bendersky
Onkul
Andemin P.
Victoria L.
Faizabad
Khairabad
Chakaran
Gharan
Kala Panja
Sarhad
Bozai Gumbaz
Jirm
Ishkashim
Kala Sist
Babatangi
Baroghil
Darkot P.
Darband
Zebak
Khotagan P.
Nushau
Mir Wali
Dalti
Karambar
HUNZA OR KANJUT
Khaibar
Hunza
Nagar
Yasin 7770
Mastuj
Tirich Mir
Agram P.
Dora P.
Lapis Lazuli (Mines)
Kala Drasan
Laspur
Shandur P.
Pingal
Gupis
Pandar L.
Chitral
Gilgit
GILGIT
Shia P.
Barak
Faraj Khan
Panchgram
Shu
Pashil
Badamak
Bros
Kala Drosh
Tal P.
Palesar P.
Chachi P.
Khanbari P.
Kinijut P.
Kani P.
Sazin
Indus
Chilas
Kalam
Korang
Kotgala
Lamuti
KAFIRISTAN
Kashkar Valley

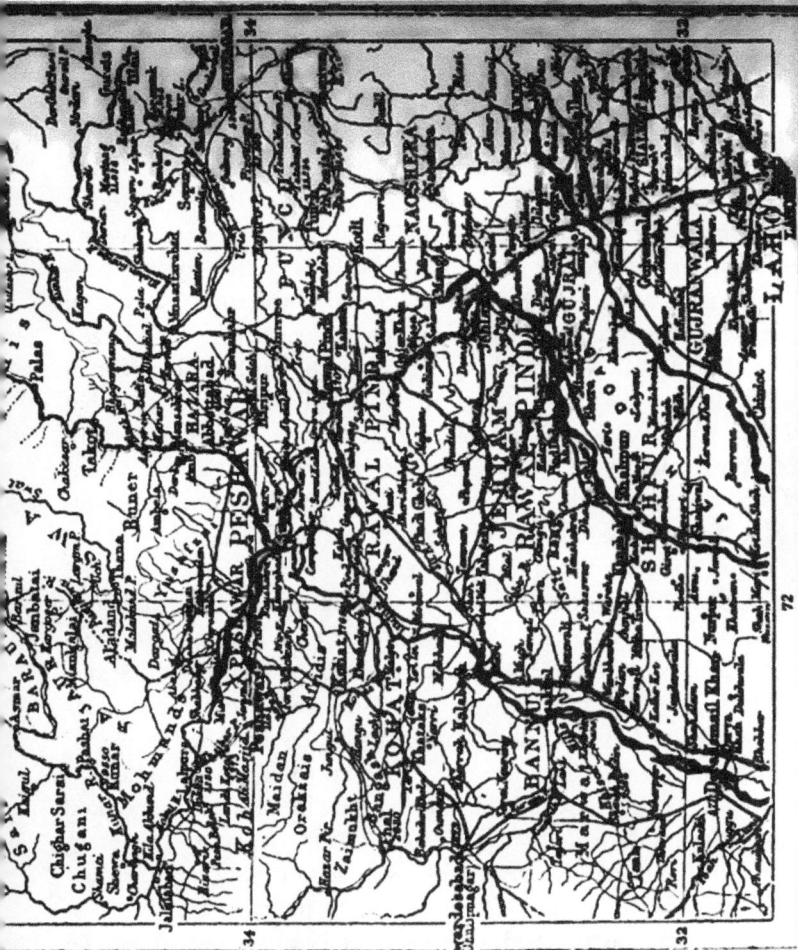

MAP OF NORTHERN FRONTIER OF THE PUNJAB.

English Miles

from the Government of India and from the Maharajah of Kashmir in return for his acknowledgment of suzerainty. As the Pathans say, *"Brotherly love is all very well, but let there be some sort of an account kept."* In 1886, and again in 1888, he sent two of his sons, Afzul-ul-Mulk and Nizam-ul-Mulk, down into India. They came back much impressed with what they had seen, and did all they could to strengthen the alliance of their father with the Great *Sircar*, (the name by which the Indian Government is known to the natives all over India), in spite of the strong anti-English faction that had sprung up in Chitral. Aman-ul-Mulk died very suddenly.

He was an old man, and all the circumstances of his death indicated that he had succumbed in the ordinary course of nature to a sudden attack of illness, but it is so unusual in Chitral for the *mehtar* to come to a peaceful end, that most of the Chitralis believe that he was poisoned. Nizam-ul-Mulk was away from Chitral at the time. He was in Yasin, of which he was the Governor, and the *mehtarship* was seized by his brother Afzul; Nizam taking refuge with the British agent in Gilgit. Afzul-ul-Mulk was anxious to draw still closer the ties that bound him to the English, and asked that an officer might be sent to reside permanently in Chitral. Before, however, any arrangement could be made he was killed, after a reign of a very few months, by his uncle, Sher Afzul, who, coming up stealthily from Cabul, attacked the fort by night, and killed him during the *mêlée*.

Nizam-ul-Mulk at once hurried to Chitral from Gilgit, and succeeded in ousting Sher Afzul, who again fled to Cabul, and Nizam-ul-Mulk became *mehtar*. He was an agreeable, cultivated man, with many European tastes, but he was weak, and not of good character even according to Chitrali ideas, and his habit of drinking to excess alienated from him the more fanatical of his subjects, to whom, being Mahommedans, wine is strictly forbidden. He, like his brother, asked that a political officer might reside in Chitral territory; and Captain Younghusband[1] with an escort of Sikhs, was accordingly sent to Mastuj, which is a fort in Upper Chitral sixty-six miles to the north of Chitral itself. This was in 1893, directly after Nizam's accession. The arrangement worked well, and in November of last year the *mehtar*, probably not feeling himself very secure, begged that the headuarters of the resident political officer, who happened at that time to be Lieu-

---

1. *The Story of the Guides* by G. J. Younghusband, the exploits of the soldiers of the famous Indian Army Regiment from the northwest frontier 1847-1900 also published by Leonaur.

tenant Gurdon, might be shifted from Mastuj to Chitral. But while the question was still under determination, the *mehtar* was murdered.

There is a quaint Afghan proverb that kings sleep upon an antheap. They certainly do in Chitral. The history of the succession is one long record of treachery and assassination. Nizam-ul-Mulk, who with all his faults was not a cruel man like his father, had neglected to put to death his younger brother Amir-ul-Mulk. He had not even sent him into exile, and in due time he reaped the reward of his forbearance, or as the Chitralis would deem it, of his folly, by falling a victim himself. On the 1st January, 1895, he was hawking with Amir-ul-Mulk at Bros, a lovely wooded village about twelve miles from Chitral. His turban fell off, and he stooped to pick it up. As he bent forward, Amir-ul-Mulk tried to shoot him. His gun missed fire, but at a signal from his master one of his retainers shot the *mehtar* in the back, and he died almost at once. The Chitralis who were present threw their caps into the air, and with wild acclamations hailed the murderer as his successor.

There is little doubt that the assassination was carefully planned. It had most probably been arranged in concert with Umra Khan, the chief of Jandol, with whom Amir-ul-Mulk had recently been staying, and with whom he is connected, Umra Khan having married a daughter of the old *mehtar* Aman-ul-Mulk. She, with Amir-ul-Mulk and the present little *mehtar*, Shuja-ul-Mulk, being his children by his Pathan wife, the daughter of the *Khan* of Asmar. It is a little difficult to follow the relationships of the different *mehtars*, but they can be understood at once from the following genealogy:—

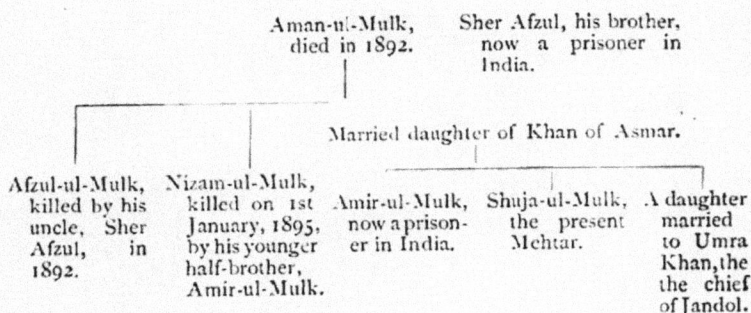

Aman-ul-Mulk, died in 1892.			Sher Afzul, his brother, now a prisoner in India.
	Married daughter of Khan of Asmar.		
Afzul-ul-Mulk, killed by his uncle, Sher Afzul, in 1892.	Nizam-ul-Mulk, killed on 1st January, 1895, by his younger half-brother, Amir-ul-Mulk.	Amir-ul-Mulk, now a prisoner in India.	Shuja-ul-Mulk, the present Mehtar.	A daughter married to Umra Khan, the the chief of Jandol.

CHITRAL FORT, SHOWING BAZAAR AND POLITICAL OFFICER'S HOUSE
IN THE DISTANCE.

It is not improbable that Sher Afzul was also a party to the plot, and that he and Umra Khan intended to make use of Amir-ul-Mulk as a catspaw. But it is a hopeless task to try and unravel the skein of Oriental intrigue, and this is mere conjecture. In justice to Umra Khan it must be frankly admitted that there is no evidence of complicity against him either. It has been taken for granted that he was concerned in the murder, because Amir-ul-Mulk had recently been staying with him, but so far as I have been able to ascertain, there is no direct proof that he instigated it. Amir-ul-Mulk hurried back at once from Bros to Chitral, and demanded recognition from Lieutenant Gurdon, who, as I have mentioned, was at that time acting as assistant British agent in Chitral. That he was in Chitral itself, and not in Mastuj, was most unfortunate, and requires a moment's explanation. Mr. Udney, the Commissioner of Peshawur, was at Asmar with the Sipah Salar, the commander-in-chief of the *amir's* army, engaged upon the work of the Afghan delimitation Commission.

There is a district called Narsat on the Kunar River, lying between Chitral and Asmar, which is claimed both by the *amir* and by the *mehtar*, and Mr. Udney had asked that Gurdon might join him at Asmar, to assist in the work of delimitation, and he was in Chitral with an escort of only eight Sikhs, waiting for the completion of certain final arrangements before starting. When Amir-ul-Mulk came to him, he very properly said that he had no power to grant recognition until instructed to do so by the Government of India. Thereupon Amir-ul-Mulk intercepted his letter to Mr. Robertson,[2] the British agent in Gilgit, and said it should not go until Gurdon promised that he should be recognised. Gurdon told him that even if such a promise were given it would not be binding on the Government of India, but that in all probability he would be recognised, as the Government made it a rule never to interfere in the private affairs of Chitral, "but," he added, "it will certainly prejudice the Government against you if you show suspicion and distrust of them by stopping my letters now."

It was a moment of great peril. Amir-ul-Mulk, who is of weak intellect, was in a state of frenzied excitement, almost bordering upon insanity; moreover he was in the hands of a knot of men bitterly opposed to English influence in Chitral, and an incautious act or word might have been productive of the most fatal results. Gurdon had only eight men with him, and if they had been attacked, all they could have done would have been to sell their lives as dearly as possible.

2. Later Sir George Robertson, K.C.S.I.

But he acted throughout with the greatest coolness and tact. He met Amir-ul-Mulk and his adherents time after time in durbar, to which he went unarmed as though unconscious of danger, for at the least sign of suspicion or distrust Amir-ul-Mulk would have jumped to the conclusion that there was no hope of his being recognised, and that he had better make sure of his revenge while Gurdon was in his power.

For a moment it seemed almost that the crisis had come when Gurdon insisted that his letter should be allowed to go. A *durbar* was held, and a long and heated discussion ensued, but finally it was sent. Then a long period of suspense followed, waiting for the reply. It required a good deal of courage to give an answer that might in a moment have turned against him the scales in which life and death were trembling in the balance, but Gurdon does not seem to have hesitated for a moment. He not only insisted that his letter should be allowed to go, but he warned Amir-ul-Mulk that the government of India views with the greatest disfavour the wholesale political murders that so generally follow these sudden revolutions; and his warning in all probability saved the lives of a number of people; the only victims being a man, against whom Amir-ul-Mulk had long borne a personal grudge, and his two sons; the sons being killed first, before their father's eyes.

CHAPTER 2

Invasion of Chitral by Umra Khan

On the 8th of January, fifty men of the 14th Sikhs under Subadar Gurmokh Singh, a native officer who distinguished himself greatly during the siege, marched down from Mastuj, and joined Gurdon in Chitral. For the benefit of those who have not been in India, I will here explain briefly who the Sikhs are, who played so important a part in the events that followed. They are almost entirely composed of Jats, who are a race apart and distinct from all other races in India. It is supposed that they are descended from the Getae of Scythia, and that they are identical with the Jatti mentioned by Pliny. They came into India at a very early date, but they only became known as "Sikhs" and sprang into prominence as a religious sect in the early part of the sixteenth century; their founder or *guru* being a devotee called Nanak, who revolted against the idolatries practised by the Hindus, and taught that all men are equal, and that the main things necessary for true religion are a belief in one God, purity, chastity, and charity.

A century later Guru Govind, the tenth Guru, goaded by the persecutions of the Mogul Emperors, formed his followers into a militant sect, bound together by a fierce hatred of all Mahommedans, changing their name from "*Sikhs*," "disciples," into "*Singhs*," "lions." They are not allowed to smoke, or to cut their hair, and they must wear steel on some part of their bodies. They generally wear it in the form of a *quoit* fastened into the turban, steel being to them the emblem of that strength by which alone they think that happiness can be secured upon this troubled earth. Guru Govind's invocation, in compliance with which they carry steel always upon them, shows how sedulously the warrior spirit has been fostered runs thus:—

The protection of the infinite Lord is over us.

17

Subadar Gurmokh Singh

Thou art the Lord—the cutlass, the knife, and the dagger.
The protection of the immortal being is over us.
The protection of All-Steel is constantly over us.

Of all the native races with whom we have had to contend, the Sikhs have been the hardest to subdue, but have been the best and most faithful of our soldiers when subdued. Unlike the Pathan, who fights best when victory seems assured, the Sikh shows to most advantage in the desperate moments of a struggle against overwhelming odds. He has proved this in many a stubborn fight, and never more so than in the defence of the fort at Chitral.

On the 1st of February, the British agent arrived from Gilgit, after a cold and difficult march over the Shandur Pass. He had with him an escort commanded by Captain Townshend of the Central Indian Horse, composed of two hundred and eighty men of the 4th Kashmir Rifles (Imperial Service Troops) and thirty-three men of the 14th Sikhs under Lieutenant Harley. Unfortunately there were no guns. If there had been, it seems likely from the light of subsequent events that there would have been no siege, for neither the Chitralis nor the Pathans seem able to stand against artillery fire. They are not accustomed to it, and it seems to demoralise them altogether. That at least was found to be the case both at Chaklewat and at Nisagol. With Mr. Robertson were also Captain Campbell of the Central Indian Horse, the Inspecting Officer of the Kashmir Imperial Service Troops, and Surgeon-Captain Whitchurch; Captain Baird of the 24th Punjab Infantry, the military assistant to the British agent, arriving a day or two later. On the 10th of February, hearing that Umra Khan had taken Kila Drosh, Mr. Robertson deemed it advisable to move into the fort.

Up to that time Gurdon and his escort had occupied a large house known as the Political Officer's house, which during the siege became the headquarters of Sher Afzul. The occupation of the fort was an absolutely necessary precaution, the political officer's house being quite unsuitable for defence, but it greatly intensified the bitter feeling against us, Amir-ul-Mulk declaring that never before had such an insult been offered to the ladies of the *mehtar's* household, who have their apartments in the fort.

Amir-ul-Mulk, finding that he was hated and despised by the Chitralis, soon after the murder of his brother had written to Umra Khan begging that he would come to his assistance; and early in February that redoubtable chieftain, in spite of the heavy snow and severe

THE LOWARAI PASS

weather, made his way across the Lowarai Pass, which separates Dir from Chitral, losing many men on the way from frostbite and exposure. He then found his further progress barred by the strong fort of Drosh on the Chitral frontier. The Chitralis hate the Pathans, and were by no means inclined to acquiesce tamely in the invitation of Amir-ul-Mulk, who, finding this to be the case, wrote to Umra Khan and asked him to retire again to Jandol. Umra Khan very naturally replied that since he had come so far, and had given himself so much trouble, he should remain; and he thereupon invested Kila Drosh, which after a few days was surrendered to him by the treachery of the governor. This was the position of affairs when the British agent arrived in Chitral.

He wrote at once to Umra Khan to proceed no further into Chitral territory, and to retire forthwith from Kila Drosh. This warning Umra Khan disregarded altogether, and on February 14th Mr. Robertson sent down Captain Townshend to Gairat, which is halfway between Chitral and Drosh, with eighty *sepoys* and seven signallers, to form a post of observation, and to instil courage into the Chitralis, who had become disheartened by the capture of Drosh and the near approach of Umra Khan. On February 23rd Sher Afzul, who since his flight from Chitral in 1892 had been detained in Cabul by the *amir* under an understanding with the Government of India that he should not be allowed to leave Afghanistan, but who had succeeded in effecting his escape with a number of the Chitralis who had shared his fortunes and followed him into exile, arrived in Drosh and joined Umra Khan.

His arrival greatly augmented the danger of a situation that was already sufficiently full of peril. Mr. Robertson wrote again to Umra Khan telling him that the orders of the Government of India must be obeyed, and that he must leave Chitral territory without any further delay, and that if he did not do so he, the British agent, would assist the Chitralis to make him go. To this warning also Umra Khan paid no attention, and, his conduct being reported by Mr. Robertson to the Government of India, they perceived the very critical nature of the situation, and on March 22, 1895, issued the following proclamation to the peoples of Swat and Bajour:—

Be it known to you, and any other persons concerned that Umra Khan, Chief of Jandol, in spite of repeated assurances of friendship to the British Government, and regardless of frequent warnings to refrain from interfering with the affairs of Chitral, which is a protected state under the suzerainty of Kashmir, has forcibly entered the Chitral valley, and has attacked the Chitrali people. The Government of India have now given Umra Khan full warning that unless he retires from Chitral by the 1st April, corresponding with the 1st day of *Showar* 1312H., they will use force to compel him to do so. In order to carry out this purpose they have arranged to assemble on the Peshawur border a force of sufficient strength to overcome all resistance, and to march through Umra Khan's territory towards Chitral.

The sole object of the Government of India is to put an end to the present, and to prevent any future unlawful aggression in Chitral territory; and as soon as this object has been attained, the force will be withdrawn. The Government of India have no intention of permanently occupying any territory through which Umra Khan's misconduct may now force them to pass, or of interfering with the independence of the tribesmen so long as they on their part refrain from attacking or impeding in any way the march of the troops. Supplies and transport will be paid for, and all persons are at liberty to pursue their ordinary avocations in perfect security.

Mr. Robertson's letter necessarily took some time to reach India, and long before the date of this proclamation hostilities had begun. The arrival of Sher Afzul completely altered the position of affairs, for until then the bulk of the Chitralis were quite as anxious as the British agent to prevent Umra Khan from entering Chitral. When however, Umra Khan was joined by Sher Afzul whom they would have much rather had for *mehtar* than Amir-ul-Mulk, they not only withdrew all opposition, but made common cause with him. The difficulty in the way of an amicable arrangement was this. Both Sher Afzul and Amir-ul-Mulk were anxious to be recognised as *mehtar*, and that at once, and Mr. Robertson had no power to recognise either without definite instructions from the Government of India. There can be no doubt that Sher Afzul would have been the better man to support, and Mr. Robertson seems to have felt this to be the case, for he wrote a very friendly letter to him, saying that he would be glad to see him and discuss matters amicably, and that he thought it most probable that the Government of India would be willing to recognise him. It is true that Amir-ul-Mulk had been temporarily and provisionally recognised, but it was found that he had been treacherously corresponding with Umra Khan, and it was impossible that he should be allowed to remain on the throne any longer.

Unfortunately, from the time that Sher Afzul joined Umra Khan he seems to have been virtually a prisoner in his hands, and it was not at all to the latter's liking that Sher Afzul should be allowed quietly to assume the *mehtarship*, whilst he himself was obliged to retire ignominiously to Jandol without reaping any profit from his foray either in territory or plunder. Instead therefore of Sher Afzul going himself to meet Mr. Robertson, one of his followers, Sayid Ahmed, was sent to do so. He was most insolent both in manner and in the nature of his demands. He insisted that Sher Afzul should be at once unconditionally recognised as *mehtar*, that the British troops should retire to Gilgit, and that for the future only a native agent should reside in Chitral, as in the time of Aman-ul-Mulk. If these terms were not agreed to he said that Sher Afzul would not be able to prevent Umra Khan from invading Chitral.

At the very time this interview was taking place, men were being secretly sent to break down the road between Chitral and Mastuj. This shows that it was intended to allure the British force, if a retirement had been agreed to, into a trap where they could have been surrounded and annihilated without difficulty. Indeed it was afterwards discovered that Amir-ul-Mulk, who was with the British agent in the fort, had arranged that if Mr. Robertson could be induced to retire to Gilgit, he would himself attack him at the Bitari Pari between Chitral and Mastuj. Between thirty and forty years ago Golab Singh, the *Maharajah* of Kashmir, sent a force of three thousand men under General Phup Singh to attack Gor Rahman, the Rajah of Hunza. They were inveigled, on to a dreadful "*pari*" not far from Bunji, which is still known as the "Phup Singh Pari," and the whole of the three thousand men, with the exception of fifty or sixty who were made prisoners and sold into slavery, were cut to pieces. A "*pari*" is a place where the road comes to a sheer precipice overhanging the river, across which a road has to be built out upon piles driven into the face of the cliff.

There is a decrepit old man now, (as at time of first publication), in Gupis who is one of the few survivors of that massacre. He is quite blind and very feeble, but he has managed to crawl down to the fort for medical treatment and help. He told me that though for years he had been known by his Mahommedan name of Mahbah Shah, he was really a Dogra Brahmin called Devi Dass, and one of Golab Singh's *sepoys*. He said that they had no guns with them, and only three days' ra-

23

"PARI" TWO MILES NORTH OF KILA DROSH

tions, and that being so large a force they were over-confident. When they got on to the "*pari*" they found that the enemy, who were about six thousand strong, were in front of them, and had also blocked the way behind and above them, and there was no possible means of getting away. For ten days they had neither food nor water. Then the enemy held a conference with their officers, and swore an oath on the *Koran* that they would not touch them if they would give up their arms and baggage—so they piled them all up in a heap, and the enemy came and took them away.

After that they surrounded them, and waited for a few days more until they were utterly exhausted with hunger and incapable of resisting, and then killed all but sixty who were made Mahommedans and sold into slavery. He himself was taken down to Tongir, and was a slave there for many years. Then his master took him to Yasin, and sold him to the late *mehtar*, Nizam-ul-Mulk, who sent him to Chitral, where he worked for many years in the fields, being chained up at night so that he should not escape. Finally he managed to get across into Badakshan, and lived there as a woodcutter until he became blind; then hearing that the English had come to Gupis he came over in the hope that they might be able to cure him.

The same fate befell Captain Ross and the detachment of the 14th Sikhs he was bringing down from Mastuj, and the same fate would probably have befallen the Chitral garrison had they left the fort. They had no guns, and it was the guns and the guns only that enabled Colonel Kelly to force his way through from Gilgit in the face of a confident and conquering enemy.

Fortunately the question of retirement was never for a moment contemplated by Mr. Robertson. He felt that, however desirable it might have been under other circumstances for Sher Afzul to have become *mehtar*, it was not possible to accede to terms dictated in so arrogant a manner; and all who know anything of Orientals will acknowledge that he acted wisely in declining even to consider the question. As for Amir-ul-Mulk, he had shown himself quite unfit for rule. He had made himself hateful to the Chitralis, and had been guilty of treachery to the English. Mr. Robertson therefore declared that, subject to the approval of the Government of India, Shuja-ul-Mulk, his younger brother, was recognised as *mehtar*.

The law of succession in Chitral is peculiar. The claimant must not only be legitimately descended from a previous *mehtar*, but his father must himself have actually been on the throne. The only persons then

AMIR–UL–MULK, GUARDED BY SOLDIERS OF THE 14TH SIKHS

living who fulfilled these conditions, and who would have been acknowledged by the Chitralis were Sher Afzul, Amir-ul-Mulk, and the little Shuja-ul-Mulk. Although they are own brothers, Shuja-ul-Mulk is not lacking in intellect like Amir-ul-Mulk, but is a bright intelligent lad about twelve years old, who bids fair to turn out a strong and capable ruler. Already he takes a keen interest in all matters of state, and has a natural kingliness of manner, with a sedate gravity that is remarkable in one so young, and not a little pathetic. Poor boy—he no doubt feels that the abhorred Fury with the shears is nearer to him than to other boys of his age, and that he, at any moment, may share the fate of his brothers.

The scene at the *durbar* on the 2nd March, when he was declared to be *mehtar*, was exceedingly dramatic and impressive, and the quiet dignified grace with which he received the homage of the attendant nobles is said to have been most striking. The British agent said that as he was so young he would require the assistance of a council of greybeards, and Captain Townshend, for whom he seems to have a real affection, was made responsible for his personal safety. In the evening a number of prominent people came to render him homage, salutes were fired, and the wild march played which the Chitralis always use on the accession of a new *mehtar*. Mr. Robertson then wrote to Sher Afzul that Shuja-ul-Mulk having been definitely recognised as *mehtar*, he must either leave Chitral territory at once or must come in and acknowledge him. Under all the circumstances a wiser choice could not have been made, and the courage and resource shown by Mr. Robertson not only during the siege itself, but during the terribly anxious month that preceded it, compel the warmest admiration.

CHAPTER 3

Lord Elgin's Speech

The critical nature of the situation is brought out very clearly in the speech made by Lord Elgin, the Viceroy of India, on the 29th March. Speaking in the Supreme Legislative Council, he said:—

> At the time of the murder of Nizam-ul-Mulk, in January last. Lieutenant Gurdon, the political officer, was on a visit to Chitral with an escort of only ten men. By great prudence and tact he avoided any collision with Amir-ul-Mulk and his party, and the arrival of a reinforcement of fifty men from Mastuj enabled him to maintain his position till he was joined, on February 1st, by Dr. Robertson, the British agent at Gilgit. That Lieutenant Gurdon's position was one of danger was realised by Dr. Robertson and by the Government of India from the moment that they received the news of Nizam-ul-Mulk's murder. It was impossible for him to withdraw with safety.
>
> On January 8th, Dr. Robertson wrote to Lieutenant Gurdon:—
>
> > If there is any prospect of trouble, sit tight, and send off urgent messengers to Mastuj Ghizar, and do not commit yourself and your escort to that terrible road along the left bank of the river between Mastuj and Chitral.
>
> Recent events have only too terribly confirmed the wisdom of that advice. It was, therefore, essential that he should be supported or be relieved in some manner. It was also considered by the Government to be desirable that Dr. Robertson should go to Chitral to endeavour to bring about a peaceful solution of the succession—a very difficult task, for which his experience specially qualified him. He was instructed to report to the

KILA DROSH

Government of India what claimant would be most acceptable to the people.

All this was in the regular course of business, but at this point Umra Khan appeared on the scene, perhaps as a partner in the plot for the murder of the *mehtar*, but at all events as an aggressor who laid siege to the frontier fort of Kila Drosh. There is no community between the people of Bajaur and the tribes subject to the *Mehtar* of Chitral, who are different in race, in sentiment, and in character. Umra Khan has entertained for some years past aggressive designs upon Chitral, and has openly acknowledged his enmity with the ruling family. The Government of India have had, on several occasions since 1891, to warn Umra Khan that aggression in Chitral would be regarded with disfavour.

Umra Khan could make no pretence of a right to interfere in the Chitral succession. He had acknowledged the relative positions of Chitral and the Government of India, when in 1890 he himself applied to the Government of India to mediate between him and Chitral in regard to their respective claims to land which, however, he subsequently occupied by force when the old *mehtar*, Amir-ul-Mulk, died in 1892. On the occasion of making his present invasion into Chitral territory, he represented in writing to the officers of the Government that he had no design of interfering in the business of government, but that Amir-ul-Mulk had opposed his wishes, and he had been compelled to become his enemy.

Still the fact remains that it was in defiance of warnings that he came, and it is in defiance of renewed warnings that he still remains. Umra Khan was joined, about the 24th of February, by Sher Afzul. This man is a brother of the former *mehtar*, Amir-ul-Mulk, and therefore uncle to the last two rulers. He had long been a refugee from Chitral in Badakshan, whence he made a sudden raid on Chitral, in November 1892, killed his nephew Afzal-ul-Mulk, and usurped the power. His rule was short, for when Nizam-ul-Mulk advanced, on December 1st, 1892, he had not sufficient support to hold his own, and fled to Cabul, whence he has now reappeared as a claimant for the *mehtarship*.

There is reason to believe that he has by no means the unanimous support of the people, but under certain circumstances he might have proved an acceptable candidate. He has, however, come with the open support of Umra Khan, has identified himself with the defiance of the Government of India, and has sent an insolent letter to the British agent requiring the withdrawal of all British officers from Chitral, and threatening an advance of Umra Khan's troops should they not be withdrawn.

It has been necessary to say this much to enable a just view to be formed of the circumstances. Dr. Robertson, in the exercise of his duty as the representative of the suzerain power, is at present in Chitral. Under all ordinary circumstances the forces and supplies at Gilgit would have sufficed for the maintenance of peace and of our proper influence and position, but the circumstances are not normal. The presence of Umra Khan has disturbed the calculations on which the existing arrangements were based. I can best describe the effect of the invasion in Dr. Robertson's own words. Writing from Mastuj on January 28th, he said:—

Umra Khan invested Kila Drosh on the 26th. and has effected a complete change in the situation. All Chitralis are united to resist Umra Khan.

In the same letter he said:

Gurdon cannot withdraw from Chitral without our help, and if he made any sign of retiring we should be mobbed and overwhelmed by crowds of fugitives. Chitral is in a state of panic. We cannot get to Chitral before the 31st. Umra Khan is credited with a desire to arrest Gurdon by some people.

When we get to Chitral the situation is not much better, except that Gurdon will be safe if Umra Khan advances rapidly with the most overwhelming force: even then we can hardly retire with prudence, the road is so terribly bad. Supplies, if they can be purchased, cannot be brought in at present, as all men are away fighting. My present idea, subject to subsequent alteration or modification, is to try and get to Chitral and hold the fort there to the bitter end if necessary. If Umra Khan fails at Kila Drosh, or makes no further advance, it is only the supply question which should then trouble us.

The fall of Kila Drosh still further accentuated the difficulty. Up till then Dr. Robertson had, after reaching Chitral, maintained most scrupulously the attitude of non-interference prescribed by his instructions in spite of repeated requests from the Chitralis. But when Umra Khan had thus committed himself to an act of open hostility, the Government of India felt that, however unwilling they might be to recognise Amir-ul-Mulk as *mehtar*, he was there *de facto*, and they were bound to authorise Dr. Robertson to give the Chitralis such material and moral support as was necessary to repel the invaders, and they at the same time gave orders for the reinforcement of the various garrisons, so far as troops were available in the Gilgit district. I was a little sorry to hear the remark made by the hon. member which might be taken—though I am sure he did not so mean it—as somewhat disparaging to our officers in the Gilgit district. I have before me a list of those officers, and it contains many names of men who, though perhaps comparatively young, have seen much service of the kind they are now called upon to perform, and they have been especially selected for the present duty.

We are not able at present to write the history of recent events, but we do know that in a moment of emergency Lieutenant Gurdon, one of these officers, not only kept his head, but showed a courage and resource that would have done credit to the most experienced. I should also mention that Colonel Kelly, commanding the Pioneer Regiment, the senior officer, is now in military command. The orders for the reinforcement of the garrisons issued from Calcutta on February 19th, before Sher Afzul had appeared on the scene, and when the matter before Dr. Robertson and the Government of India was the rendering of assistance to Chitral in protecting the country from an invader, not the support of one candidate against another, it soon became apparent that further measures were necessary, and when, after March 1st, all communication with Dr. Robertson ceased, the Government of India were forced to review the position.

Shortly it was this, that Dr. Robertson, our duly accredited agent who had been obliged to push on to Chitral, as I have stated, by the paramount necessity of securing Lieutenant Gurdon's safety, was himself cut off by some agency of which we knew little, but which could scarcely be other than hostile. We knew that

Dr. Robertson did not regard himself in any immediate danger. He held the fort, a strong position, with about 300 men, and he said that any attack on the fort was 'as improbable as its accomplishment would be impossible.' But his communications being cut off, any attempt to replenish his supplies was a very difficult operation: how difficult and dangerous has since been seen.

The Government of India were bound by every consideration to relieve their officers from such a position, which, if not of immediate, was certainly one of proximate danger. Now reinforcements could not be sent by Kashmir and Gilgit, because the passes are closed by snow until June, at the earliest, when it would be too late to relieve Dr. Robertson by that circuitous route. There was but one alternative—an advance from Peshawur; and the hostile combination of Umra Khan and Sher Afzul gave an additional justification for its adoption, Jandol lies between British India and Chitral on the only road open at this time of the year, and the Government of India have come very reluctantly to the conclusion that, as Umra Khan will not listen to remonstrances, but persists in a course which must result in danger to Dr. Robertson and his party, they have a duty which they must perform, and that is by entering his territory to compel him to look to his own affairs.

On the best information available, the Government believed that Dr. Robertson's supplies ought to suffice till about the end of April, and the orders for the collection of transport issued on March 7th were calculated to enable his relief to be effected by that time. Subsequent arrangements have been made with the same object. I have no doubt that honourable members will agree that the disaster to Captain Ross's party in their attempt to reach Chitral from Mastuj has made it apparent that these orders were not issued a day too soon, and has established the necessity of the expedition.

It may be desirable to indicate the considerations which have determined the strength of the force which is being mobilised. The Government of India have proclaimed to the tribes along the Peshawur border the object with which this expedition will go forth, and that their independence is absolutely assured; and it is hoped that their concurrence will be obtained. But the Government of India cannot shut their eyes to the fact that they have to secure a long and difficult line of communications, and they are of opinion that in the interests of peace this must be held in great strength. Any resistance offered ,not merely to the fighting line, but to its supports or convoys, might leave behind fresh grounds of quarrel; and the Government of India, while they must push on to their goal and insist by force if necessary upon the removal of the hostile aggression which menaces their officers in Chitral, desire above all things to avoid any step which may lead to any extension of the frontiers of British India or any interference with the independence of the tribes. For the attainment of these objects it is necessary not only to use every effort to convince the tribes of our friendly intentions to them, but also to advance—now that an advance has become inevitable—in such force as to make it evident that any hostility on their part could be instantly and effectually crushed.

I hope that hon. members will admit that in laying before them the information in my possession, and the object of the Government, I have spoken with the utmost frankness. I am not going to obscure what I have endeavoured to make clear by being drawn into a disquisition on frontier policy, which might not in any event be very appropriate in this Council, certainly never so inappropriate as now. For the present we have before us a single issue, the claim of brave men, British and Indian, who have not flinched in the performance of their duty, to the support of their countrymen in their hour of need. It is a claim that I believe will go straight home to every British and Indian heart, that will inspire our counsels with unanimity, and will quicken the step of every man whose duty calls him forth on this expedition.

CHAPTER 4

Reconnaissance of March 3rd

In this speech Lord Elgin mentions that all communications from
Chitral had ceased since the 1st March. The reason was that the siege
began on the 3rd. Late in the day on March 2nd Mr. Robertson received information that Sher Afzul had arrived in the valley in which
the fort is situated, but men sent out to make inquiries reported that
the information was false. The following day, however, news was again
brought that Sher Afzul, with an armed following, was in a small
house in a ravine about a mile and a quarter to the south of the fort.
Captain Campbell, with two hundred men of the 4th Kashmir Rifles, was sent out to make a reconnaissance. He was accompanied by
Captains Townshend and Baird, and by Surgeon-Captain Whitchurch.
Lieutenant Gurdon also went with him, and Mr. Robertson followed
shortly afterwards. Fifty men were left in the *bazaar* to hold the road,
and the remainder proceeded along the path leading to the political
officer's house.

A party of men, about one hundred and fifty strong, were seen
on the bare spur which forms the right bank of the ravine. Captain
Baird, with fifty *sepoys*, was detached to watch them, while the rest
of the troops, then reduced to one hundred, advanced steadily in the
direction where Sher Afzul's force was said to be. Although the party
opposed to Captain Baird's detachment carried banners, it was the
opinion of the political news-writer in Chitral—Jemadar Rab Nawaz
Khan—a native officer of the 15th Bengal Lancers, who had been
many years in Chitral, and who knew the people intimately—that
it was a mere piece of bravado, and that no serious advance was intended. To test the point a single shot was fired over the heads of the
men on the hill, who at once opened a heavy fire on Captain Baird's
party, while Captain Townshend, who in the meantime had crossed

the open ground leading to the hamlet before mentioned, became engaged with an enemy invisible indeed, but evidently in considerable strength, for their fire was hot and furious.

It was subsequently discovered that very shortly after Captain Campbell's party left the fort, and before other hostilities began, the Danin men opened fire on the fort from across the river, and wounded a *sepoy*. Captain Baird then advanced across the mouth of the ravine, and charged up the spur on the right bank, the enemy retreating before him, firing as they went. Captain Baird fell mortally wounded, and Lieutenant Gurdon, who had carried a message to him from Captain Campbell, assumed command of the party. But the enemy, though retreating up the hill, were not defeated. They descended into the ravine, and crossed over to the left bank quitted by Captain Baird and his men, taking Lieutenant Gurdon in rear. In the meantime affairs had not been going well with Captain Townshend's party. He had advanced up to within two hundred yards of the hamlet, keeping his men as much as he could under the cover of a small revetted bank. The volley firing made no impression on the enemy, who kept on advancing and overlapping him on both flanks. Sher Afzul's men were well armed, numerous, and skilful with the rifle. They took cover, too, in a perfectly marvellous way, and there was seldom anything for our men to fire at except puffs of smoke emerging from behind stones or from the side of trees.

Captain Campbell then ordered a charge with the bayonet to clear the hamlet. It was gallantly led by Captain Townshend, General Baj Singh, and Major Bhikam, but it could not be carried home, the terrain being entirely open and devoid of cover, and the fire of the enemy being steady, well aimed, and continuous. Two of their leaders. General Baj Singh and Major Bhikam, were killed at once, and many *sepoys*. It was found, too, on getting up to within forty yards of the hamlet, which was concealed in a grove of trees, that it was in reality a large village with a wall over three hundred feet in length, behind which the enemy were ensconced, and which afforded the most complete shelter. There was nothing for it but to retreat. Captain Campbell at this moment was shot in the knee, and Captain Townshend assumed the command. He had Captain Campbell and Major Bhikam carried to the rear, and then retired the men by alternate parties, one half being ordered to keep up a hot fire on the loopholes of the hamlet, whilst the other half ran off in twos and threes to more sheltered ground.

The retreat was conducted very slowly and deliberately, though the enemy, who came running out, soon overlapped the little column on both flanks, some even getting behind it, whilst little knots of fanatical swordsmen from time to time charged furiously down upon it. The native hospital assistant, Bhowani Dass, dressed Captain Campbell's wound upon the field, and almost immediately afterwards was shot through the head and killed. When the polo ground was reached, the firing became still hotter, the houses and walls to the west being lined with Chitralis, hitherto supposed to be friendly, but who now at the first sign of a British reverse went over to the other side; partly, no doubt, from a secret dislike to the English, but chiefly to obtain the favour of the conquering Sher Afzulites.

From all the hamlets as they approached the fort they were fired at from behind the shelter of orchards and houses—from right and left, front and rear. There was nothing; for it but to double. But there was no panic or unsteadiness, and Townshend was able to rally his *sepoys* without difficulty at a small hamlet, where he found the British agent steadying and encouraging a few men whom he had gathered together. A message had been sent to Lieutenant Harley in the fort to bring out fifty of the Sikhs, and to the steady behaviour of these splendid soldiers, and to the coolness and gallantry of Captain Townshend, must be attributed the fact that the retreat did not degenerate into a rout, and the rout into a massacre.

It was nearly eight o'clock before the fort was reached, and in the dim light it was difficult to distinguish the enemy from the retreating *sepoys*. Harley therefore ordered the men not to fire, but to kneel down with fixed bayonets by the side of a wall about half a mile from the fort. They were under a heavy dropping fire all the time, and the temptation to return it must have been very great, but not a man fired. There could not be a more severe test than this of coolness and discipline. While all this was going on, Gurdon, with his detachment of fifty men and the dying Captain Baird, was still away on the steep hillside to the right. Whitchurch, who had hurried to the assistance of Baird, was sent to take him to the rear, and Gurdon retreated slowly back to the fort, helping to cover the retreat of Townshend's men as he went.

On the way he met his *syce*, or native groom, bringing out his pony for him to ride back upon. He told him he did not require it, and to go back with it to the fort, but he was killed before he could get there. This is an instance—but by no means a solitary one—of the heroism and devotion displayed all through the siege by the native servants and followers.

Mr. Robertson, who had gone forward at the beginning of the fight to see what Captain Campbell's party were doing, and who had returned by himself across the polo ground to see that all was right in the fort, and to tell Harley to bring out his Sikhs, had a very perilous ride. He had to run the gauntlet of a heavy fire all the way, and it was marvellous that he escaped unhurt. When everyone else had come in, it was found that Baird and Whitchurch were missing, and it was supposed that they had been cut off and killed; but some time afterwards they made their appearance at the garden, and not at the main gate of the fort, poor Baird being in a dying condition. Whitchurch had placed him in a "*dooly*," or stretcher, and started for the fort, making first for the polo ground. He had with him a handful of *sepoys* of the 4th Kashmir Rifles, under the command of a native officer, a Gurkha called Bidrina Singh, and a few hospital *kahars*, or stretcher-bearers.

Matters developed so rapidly that in a very short time they were actually behind as well as between the two retreating parties around which the enemy was swarming, and when the retirement became a rapid retreat they dropped, of course, still further behind; and though the great bulk of the enemy were ahead of them, small detached parties soon became aware of their isolated position, and began to attack them on all sides. As they crossed the polo ground, three of the men who were carrying the stretcher were killed by successive shots. As each man fell, his place was at once supplied by another, but when a fourth was hit it was clear that the stretcher could no longer be carried, so Whitchurch partly carried and partly dragged Baird along the ground.

By this time they were completely cut off, the main body of the enemy lying between them and the fort, while all around them were little groups of men firing into them, and trying to make up their minds to charge home. Whitchurch was therefore compelled to make for the river bank, although the ground was very difficult. He had to charge and carry two or three stone walls, and once, when completely surrounded by the enemy, he and his gallant Gurkhas gave them such a lesson with revolver and bayonet, that they never tried close quarters again. And so at last, their number diminishing every minute, they reached the fort, where they had been given up for lost. Thirteen men in all came in, but of these only seven had fought their way through with Whitchurch, the other six being fugitives who joined him just before he reached the fort.

Of his little party nearly half were killed, but not a man had attempted to leave his officers. Baird was wounded three times, but strange to say, Whitchurch was untouched, except for a slight contusion in the foot from a spent bullet, although the last time Baird was hit, just outside the walls of the fort, his head lay upon Whitchurch's shoulder. Had it not been for the darkness which concealed them from those of the enemy who were not immediately around them, not one of them could have reached the fort alive. The brave and gentle Captain Baird died the following day, declaring himself satisfied to die the death of a soldier. His last moments were entirely occupied in describing to the British agent the way in which their retreat had been effected, and in begging him that Whitchurch's splendid gallantry might be properly and efficiently reported.

One has only to consider for a moment the desperate nature of the position in which Whitchurch and his men found themselves to appreciate the heroism of what they did. They had none of the excitement and enthusiasm of an assault to sustain their courage, but had to bear up against the long strain of a retreat under the most depressing and apparently hopeless conditions—cut off as they were from all possibility of assistance; more than a mile from the fort, in difficult ground, and unable from the darkness to see what was going on around them.

That Gurdon and they did not all come in together was due to the fact that, when Baird was wounded, Gurdon found himself confronted by a large number of the enemy, and was afraid that if he retreated at once, Whitchurch might not be able to get away. He therefore collected about a dozen men, and took up a position immediately to his front, which he held until he thought Whitchurch and Baird had had time to make good their retreat, and then fought his way slowly back to the fort. That he did not overtake them on the way was owing to Whitchurch having been obliged to leave the direct road and to make towards the river, from the bank of which he worked his way up to the fort.

The total casualties of the day were very heavy. Of the one hundred and fifty men actually engaged, twenty non-commissioned officers and men were killed and twenty-eight wounded; and of the officers, Captain Campbell was badly wounded, and Captain Baird, General Baj Singh, and Major Bhikam were killed. The enemy's strength was computed to be from one thousand to twelve hundred men, five hundred of whom were said to be Jandolis, Umra Khan's men. These were reported to be armed with Martinis, and many of the others were armed with Sniders, the remainder having matchlocks.

CHAPTER 5

Measures Adopted for Defence of Fort

On the following day, March 4th, the enemy closed in around the fort, and the siege began in earnest, the whole population of Chitral seeming to have joined Sher Afzul. Mr. Robertson, in his report to the Government, after the close of the siege, says, "Our position, though very difficult, was not hopeless till after the disaster of March 3rd, but after that unfortunate event, all the Chitralis outside the fort were compelled to join Sher Afzul for fear of their families. They also believed he was supported by the *amir*, and that Umra Khan, and the Sipah Salar, and the Mahommedans, had joined in a religious war against us, and that our position was desperate, while they knew that if in time we triumphed, they had still nothing to fear from our vengeance." Sher Afzul established his headquarters in the political officer's house, and his men also occupied the house of the news writer, Rab Nawaz Khan.

Both of these houses, and also the *serai*, or village, are within easy Martini and Snider range of the fort, which they command, being on higher ground; and from all of them a constant fusillade was maintained against the garrison whilst they were engaged in the difficult work of putting the fort into a better condition of defence. Rab Nawaz Khan, it should be mentioned, had an almost miraculous escape on the previous day. He was suddenly attacked by a number of swordsmen, cut almost to pieces, and left for dead upon the field. But during the evening, Asfandiar and Shahi-ul-Mulk, two illegitimate sons of the old *mehtar*, Amir-ul-Mulk, found that there was still life in him, and brought him secretly, under cover of the darkness, to the main gate of the fort, merely asking that if the English should eventually win the day, what they had done might be remembered in their favour. They then went back to Sher Afzul, and distinguished themselves by the ardour with which they fought against us during the siege, Asfandiar in particular making especially accurate shooting from a *sungar*, or breastwork, on the Danin side of the river. It was a masterly piece of hedging, for they managed in this way to make themselves secure whichever side might win. Rab Nawaz Khan was found to be in a dreadful plight. He had no less than nineteen sword cuts, two being on the neck, one on each side, both of which only missed the carotid artery by a hairsbreadth. But the wounds were clean, as all *tulwar* wounds are, and healed rapidly; and though he has permanently lost the use of one of his arms, and feels at times a curious sensation in the head and neck, long before the siege was over he was up and about, and taking an active part in the defence.

The first thing that had to be done was of course to take stock of the stores, and estimate for how many days the garrison was rationed. This was done, and every one put on half rations; and it was calculated that they could hold out for two and a half months, or until about the middle of June. It was also found that they had 280 rounds per man of Snider ammunition for the 4th Kashmir Rifles, and 300 rounds per man of Martini ammunition for the Sikhs. Captain Campbell's wound was a bad one, the knee-cap being completely shattered, so Captain Townshend as the next senior officer assumed the command. Fortunately it was not his first experience of war: he was in the square at Abu Klea, and had served in the Hunza Nagar campaign; and, what was of infinitely more importance at the present juncture, although a cavalry officer, he had not only made a special theoretical study of fortification, but had also acquired a certain practical knowledge of it, for he was employed only last year in building the fort at Gupis.

This knowledge now stood the Chitral garrison in good stead. It is often urged that it is useless for cavalry and infantry officers to waste their time in the study of fortification, when in time of war that would always be the work of the engineers. For countries whose outstanding possessions do not necessitate the posting of their officers in the isolated positions which the exigencies of our enormous and dispersed empire require, this argument maybe sound. In such countries they may obtain better results by specialising their abilities, for the man who devotes himself entirely to one subject must necessarily acquire a more thorough knowledge of it than one who has divided his attention amongst several. But those who have to act as pioneers and to

Chitral Fort on the banks of the Kunar River.

command the outposts of our empire ought to have a little knowledge of everything.

At the time when the fort was first occupied, on the 10th February, it was found that there was an exposed approach to the river from the water tower about thirty yards in length, so a covered way was at once built going right down into the water. All through the siege this covered way was the main object of the enemy's attack. They knew that if they could cut off the water the garrison would be reduced to the most desperate straits, and would be compelled to fight their way down to the river every time they required water. As it was, they were never in any want of it; but both the tower over the water gate and the waterway itself were under constant fire, and had to be held night and day by a strong picquet. An abutment in the south wall of the fort, overlooking the garden, was at the same time converted into a *tambour*, the garden seats being utilised to make a *banquerette* to fire from.

Until hostilities had actually commenced it was not possible to do more than this, for the worst features of the fort as a defensible position were the large number of outbuildings immediately outside the walls. These, and the walls of the garden, had now to be demolished by moonlight under a heavy fire from the enemy by the Puniali levies under Sipat Bahadur and Morad Khan, two chiefs who had accompanied Mr. Robertson from Punial, a little tributary state lying between Gilgit and Yasin. As the siege went on and weak spots were discovered, they were strengthened as far as was possible with the limited means at command. A *tambour* and *caponier* were built out in front of the main gate, effectually flanking the north face of the fort; and sweeping both it and the north and south towers. The stables, which were on the river face to the right of the water tower, were loopholed and the ends walled up. The *parados* were improved, and flanking loopholes made in the *machicoulis* galleries and in the towers.

An endeavour was also made to loophole the basement stories of the towers, but this had to be abandoned, as there was danger of disturbing the foundations. Vertical loopholes for ground fire were, however, made in the gun tower, against which the enemy showed themselves particularly active. A wall was built out from the face of the water-gate and *barbicaned*, and fireplaces were made for the *machicoulis* galleries, the wood being laid on a slab of stone, which was then pushed out upon the gallery, and which could be drawn into the embrasure of the fort when it was necessary to replenish the fire, without the men attending to it being unnecessarily exposed.

BRIDGE OVER THE CHITRAL RIVER AT DINAN, WITH FORT IN THE DISTANCE

These fires proved invaluable when repelling attacks upon dark nights when there was no moon. They projected out some feet from the wall and threw it into shadow, so that the enemy could not see what to fire at, and at the same time they lit up the ground brilliantly for some distance in front of the wall, so that the men on the ramparts were able to distinguish their assailants without difficulty, and to fire with precision and accuracy. Indeed after these fires were brought into use the night attacks, which until then had been frequent, ceased almost entirely.

Townshend also carefully inspected the towers, and found that the water tower was far too thin; so he sent up stones at night to strengthen it from the inside. He also built a cover for the *flèche* outside the water gate. But after every possible precaution had been taken, and every measure adopted that could be taken under the circumstances, and with the limited means available to the garrison, the fort still remained most unfitted in every way for purposes of defence. It is situated on low lying ground on the bank of the Chitral or Kunar River, about half a mile from the bridge at Danin, which is a strong cantilever bridge 41 yards in length and 3 yards in breadth.

It stands on the right bank of the river, which there runs roughly N. and S., the valley itself running N.E. and S.W., and is a square building of wood and stone, 80 yards in length and 25 feet in height, with a tower about 50 feet high at each corner, and a smaller tower over the water gate in the middle of the north or river face. The south face fronts towards the *serai* or village, which is about 600 yards distant, between it and the fort being open fields, but both the east and west faces are hidden by gardens and trees, and surrounded by outbuildings. On the east face there is a grove of magnificent *chenar* or sycamore trees, which grow close up to the walls of the fort, and completely overtop it. Fortunately the enemy did not attempt to construct a crow's nest in them. Had they done so they must have inflicted severe loss, and have been a terrible annoyance to the garrison.

It is difficult to understand why they omitted to do it, for the manoeuvre is one well known in Chitrali warfare, the fort at Mastuj having been taken by this means some years ago. But a far more serious defect is the position in which it stands. In the old days of matchlocks it would not have mattered, but in these days of Martini-Henrys and Sniders the whole character of hill warfare is altered. It is in a hollow in the lowest part of the valley, which does not broaden out for some way further down, and which is commanded from the hills around it from literally every point of the compass. The enemy built *sungars* or stone breastworks along the sides of these hills, and also had strong positions in the village of Danin, which is to the north of the fort on the other side of the river, and only 600 yards off; in the fortified towers at the head of the bridge, which is about the same distance away; in the house of the news-writer Rab Nawaz Khan, which is to the south-east about a thousand yards off and on higher ground than the fort which it therefore commands; in the village, which is about 600 yards up the hillside to the south; and in the political officer's house, which is still further up the hill behind it, about twelve hundred yards distant, and which is a large oblong building with a walled garden and enclosed court, standing on the high bank of a stream. Sher Afzul lived in it during the siege.

About a hundred yards behind it is a *musjid* containing the tombs of Aman-ul-Mulk, Afzul-ul-Mulk, and Nizam-ul-Mulk. The plan on the opposite page will show at a glance, how exposed the position is and what a difficult place the fort was to make defensive. It must be borne in mind too that the siege took place in March and April, when the trees were without leaves, so that they afforded little or no concealment. Any one moving about inside the fort was clearly visible to the enemy in the *sungars* on the hillsides, and it was such dangerous work going from one part of the courtyard to the other, that sheltering barricades of stones had to be erected, skirting the sides of the yard, behind which the men could take cover as they went to and from their allotted posts.

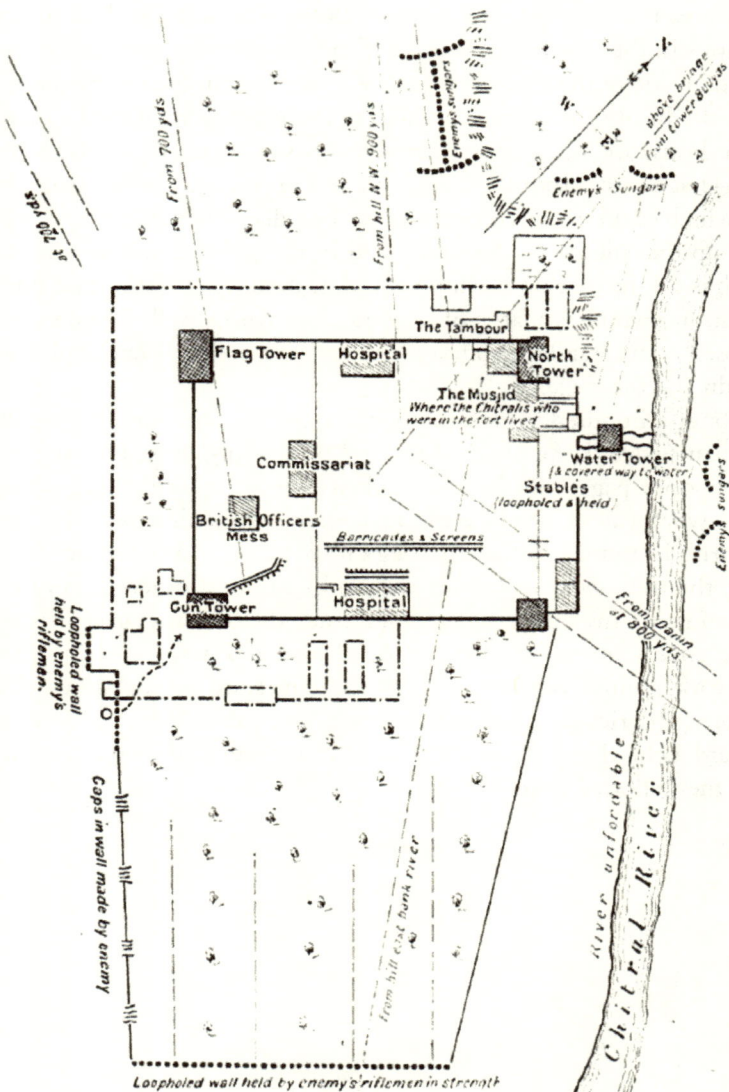

From 700 yds

qr 700 yds

From hill N.W. 900 yds

Enemy's sangars

shoot bridge from tower 840 yds

The Tambour

Flag Tower

Hospital

North Tower

The Musjid
Where the Chitralis who were in the fort lived

Water Tower
(& covered way to water)

Stables
(loopholed & held)

Commissariat

British Officers Mess

Barricades & Screens

Gun Tower

Hospital

Enemy's sangars

From Danin at 800 yds

River unfordable

Chitral River

Loopholed wall held by enemy's riflemen.

Gaps in wall made by enemy

from hill east bank river

Loopholed wall held by enemy's riflemen in strength.

Scale.

1 Inch represents about 80 Yards

Enemy's rifle fire, thus ......

Walls & buildings demolished by the garrison. thus ——————

PLAN OF THE FORT.

CHAPTER 6

Attack of March 7th on Water-Tower

On March 5th a letter was received from Umra Khan that the British troops must leave Chitral at once, that he would guarantee their safe arrival in Gilgit, and that Sher Afzul must be *mehtar*. On the following day his *diwan,* or *prime minister,* came to the fort under a flag of truce, and said that Umra Khan was the friend of the English, and that if they would evacuate the fort he would give them a safe escort to Mr. Udney at Asmar. A refusal was of course given to both proposals. As there were so few British officers, Townshend now attached Gurdon to the 4th Kashmir Rifles for duty. The next night—March 7th—the enemy made a determined effort to fire the water-tower. Underneath the tower is a narrow tunnel going down at a steep angle to the waterway. The enemy, who seemed to be about two hundred strong, brought faggots with them, and in spite of the heavy volleys that were poured down upon them from the ramparts managed under cover of the darkness to creep into the tunnel and light a large fire right underneath the tower.

They were driven out with a good deal of difficulty, and three *bheesties* or water-carriers were sent into the tunnel with *mussacks* of water to put the fire out, which they did only just in time, as it had taken a firm hold of the wooden beams. After this special precautions were taken to protect the waterway. A picquet of twenty-five men was stationed in the tower, and at night an additional picquet of twenty-five more men was placed inside the waterway also, that being the weakest and most exposed position in the fort. About sixty yards above it, the river makes a bend to the north-west towards the bridge and from the *sungars* placed at the turn of the river bank, as well as from the bridge head, there was a clear field of fire to the waterway, of which the enemy availed themselves fully. They also built two *sungars* on the opposite bank, below the village of Danin, one being only a hundred and thirty yards distant, and the other about fifty yards behind it a little further up the hill. The entrance to the waterway was at first quite unprotected, and the water-carriers were exposed to the fire from these *sungars* as soon as they came to the end of it, and began to draw water.

A barricade of stones with interstices to allow the water to flow through was therefore built out into the river, forming a very efficient screen. This of course had to be made by night. The Chitralis also kept a very careful watch on the men of the picquet as they climbed in and out of the tower. They almost always fire from rests, and take very careful aim, and very seldom waste ammunition by firing at random when they cannot see at whom they are firing. So it was found that a screen of sacking was quite a sufficient protection, for though it did not stop the bullets in the least, it concealed the men from view, and the Chitralis ceased firing at them almost entirely. Some of their shooting was wonderfully accurate. They sighted their rifles for a loophole, and when they saw a man going up into one of the towers, they waited until they thought he must have got up and would be looking out, and then fired. Several men were killed in this way.

On the night of the 13th the enemy again made an attack on the waterway, but were repelled with considerable loss. The waterway was indeed a source of constant anxiety, for between it and the trees at the north-west corner of the fort there is a stretch of about seventy yards of sandy beach lying underneath an overhanging bank, which entirely covered the beach from the fire of the fort, so that the enemy were able to get right up to the waterway without exposing themselves.

On the 14th and 15th continuous firing went on, but nothing of importance happened. On the 15th however, a letter was received from Sher Afzul saying that a party of *sepoys* had been defeated at Reshun, and on the following day he forwarded a letter from Lieutenant Edwardes stating that he and Lieutenant Fowler, R.E., with forty Kashmir Rifles and twenty Bengal Sappers, were besieged at Reshun, and that after several days' fighting they had concluded a truce with the enemy. On the same day a truce for three days was agreed to by Sher Afzul, which was afterwards extended to three days more—till the 23rd.

On the 20th, Edwardes and Fowler were brought into Sher Afzul's camp, and Mr. Robertson was allowed to send Munshi Amir Ali to talk to them. He was accompanied by one of Umra Khan's men, who

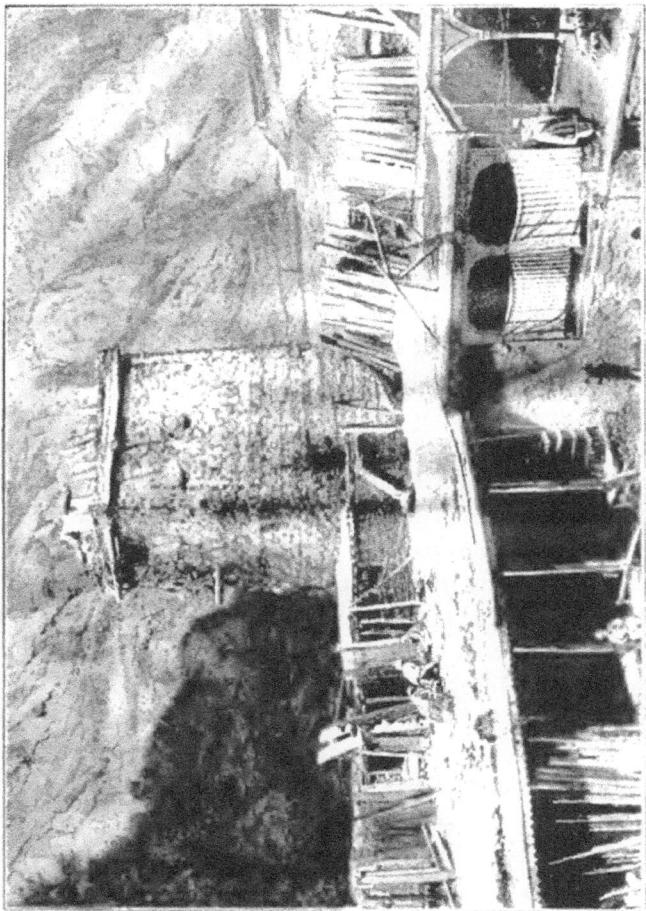

SOUTH TOWER OF CHITRAL FORT

had been a *havildar* in the 5th Punjab Infantry, and who was always employed in bringing messages to the fort, and was allowed to speak to them for about twenty minutes, but only in Hindustani. On the following day food and medicine were allowed to be sent them from the fort. Rather a quaint incident now occurred. One of the Jandolis was ill, and consulted Fowler in the way natives always consult Englishmen about their ailments. Fowler sent a letter to the fort describing the man's symptoms, and Whitchurch made up some medicine and sent it out to him. The two officers explained that they had been attacked at Reshun, and, after holding out for nine days, had been treacherously made prisoners under a flag of truce by Mahomed Isa Khan, a foster-brother of Sher Afzul, Yadgar Beg, and Mahomed Afzul Beg.

Mr. Robertson thereupon wrote to Umra Khan protesting against the violation of a flag of truce, and saying that if he were a man of honour, a *khan* of lion-like mind, he would at once release his prisoners. Umra Khan, it should be mentioned, was not in Chitral and never had been. He had never left Drosh, but had sent his two lieutenants up to Chitral, Abdul Majid Khan of Sheena, his first cousin, and Abdul Ghani Khan of Shahi, in whose hands Sher Afzul seems to have been virtually a prisoner. Edwardes and Fowler in the meantime had been taken down to Drosh, and Umra Khan sent a reply from there, in which he said that he had told the sahibs that if they wished it he would send them back to the fort, but that they had declined to go. It seems that he did really make them this offer, but they asked if their *sepoys* would be allowed to go with them, and when this was refused they declined to go back by themselves.

A few days later Umra Khan, who had received disquieting news of the advance of an English force through Swat and Bajour, and that Jandol itself was threatened, made a hurried retreat over the Lowarai Pass, taking Edwardes and Fowler and the *sepoys* with him. On the 23rd March his *diwan* again came to ask whether the British agent would retire his troops through Jandol to Peshawur, and being told that he would not, the truce was declared to be at an end. The prospect for the garrison at this time looked exceedingly gloomy. They had not heard, as Umra Khan had, of the approach either of Colonel Kelly's force or of that under Sir Robert Low.

The men were beginning to suffer in health from the long confinement, from want of food, and from the terribly insanitary condition of the fort. And now that the siege seemed likely to be continued for an indefinite period, it was decided that in a very short time the rations must be still further reduced. The medical stores, too, were running out, and the scanty supply of chloroform for the wounded was rapidly diminishing, for, unfortunately, the hospital had fallen into the hands of the enemy, and all that Whitchurch had to go on with was the very small supply he had in his hospital panniers.

When Edwardes and Fowler were taken down to Drosh, Umra Khan handed the contents of the hospital over to them. "I know," he said, "that *Sahibs* find it very hard to get along without wine, and if you can find any amongst all these bottles, you are welcome to it," but there was none.

CHAPTER 7

Union Jack Hoisted

During the truce the British agent had a Union Jack made, and now, when the fortunes of the garrison seemed darkest, and the enemy were elated hy success, and by the capture of the two British officers, it was hoisted on the flag tower as a signal of defiance, and that come what might the garrison would never give in. Curiously enough, from that time things seemed to brighten with them: possibly because the determined front they displayed shook the courage of the besiegers. As the Afghans say: "*Destiny is a bridled ass. It will go wherever you lead it.*" But often and often their hearts must have sunk within them, and many a man after a weary night of watching, as he looked up at the snowy pinnacles of Tiritch Mir in the rose-red flush of dawn, must have wondered whether he would ever see another sunrise.

On the 23rd and 24th heavy rain fell, lasting continuously all day. The little *mehtar*, Shuja-ul-Mulk, who showed the greatest courage all through the siege, caused a prayer to be written in Persian by a very holy man, Mian Rahut Shah, and put up on the ramparts on the top- of a lance, and not long after the rain ceased. On the 25th an attempt was made to utilise two old brass guns made in 1839, which had been found inside the fort, but they proved to be quite useless. They had no sights, and it was impossible to aim with any kind of accuracy, and several *sepoys* were hit whilst they were being fired; so it was decided that it was not worthwhile to try them again—that it would only be exposing the men uselessly.

After the siege it was discovered that the enemy had .forged a rude gun, but they were never able to use it, as the siege was raised before it was quite completed. On the 29th March a letter came from Edwardes from Drosh, giving full details of the capture of Fowler and himself, and saying that Umra Khan was retreating to Jandol, and tak-

54

ing them with him. But Abdul Majid Khan and Abdul Ghani Khan, and three or four hundred of their Jandoli followers, still remained with Sher Afzul in Chitral, and were the very soul of the attack, for they had more courage and more resource also than the Chitralis.

Exactly a month after the siege began information was received by the British agent that a force was advancing from Gilgit, and had already arrived at Mastuj. He had felt sure that relief would be sent, but had not expected it to arrive so soon—indeed, in a few days' time, the half rations on which the garrison had subsisted since the beginning of the siege were to have been still further reduced to enable them if necessary to hold out until the middle of July. This diminution of rations was a very serious matter, and was delayed until the last possible moment. The men were already thin, and pulled down from the long strain upon half-rations, and a still further reduction would have tried them sorely.

The garrison indeed owe their very existence to Fateh-Ali-Shah, the Aksagol of Shogot, one of the principal Chitrali nobles, who was in the fort all through the siege. Before it began he helped to get them grain, and without his assistance it would not have been possible to have obtained anything like a sufficient quantity. The officers were comparatively well off. They had plenty of horse-flesh, but the *sepoys* would not eat that, and to make matters worse all the "*ghi*," or clarified butter, had run out, and "*ghi*" to a native is what meat is to a European. The men for some time had had absolutely nothing to live upon but flour. There was however a little rum and a little tea, so Townshend ordered a dram of rum per man to be served out every fourth day to the Sikhs, and a quarter of an ounce of tea every other day to the Kashmir Rifles. He also did all he could to lighten the men's duties by taking off the fort police both by day and by night, and by sending the inlying picquet round the fort only once in every two hours.

But in spite of all this, at the beginning of April there were over eighty men on the sick list. Fortunately all the officers had kept well; one of the greatest dangers in the defence being that there were so few and the strain upon them of keeping constant watch upon every point on which an attack might be made was very great. Townshend therefore divided the day into watches as on board ship, so that they were able to snatch a little rest during the day. At night they none of them slept at all, for the night attacks were those most to be feared; but it was often very hard to keep awake. The enemy almost always attacked immediately before dawn, when it was just light enough to see, so every man had to fall in at his post an hour before sunrise, and remain there until the sun was fairly up. This habit of the Pathans, of attacking just before dawn, is referred to in a ballad written some years ago by Sir Mortimer Durand, which gives so true and vivid a description of a night attack in frontier warfare that I cannot refrain from quoting a few lines of it:—

And twice five days we stood at bay behind the crumbling wall,
And still they shrunk from the one straight rush that should have finished all.
It came at last, one wintry dawn, before the break of light,
A sudden glare of beacon fires upon the southern height;
A signal shot to east and west, and then with one wild swell
Pealed up from fifty thousand throats the Ghazis' battle yell;
And the rifle flashes hemmed us round in one broad quivering ring,
And overhead in fiery gusts the lead began to sing.
And we quenched our frozen carbines in the darkness and the snow,
And waited with fast beating hearts the onset of the foe.

On April 6th the enemy was very active. They made two large *sungars* close to the main gate, the nearest being only forty yards away, and the other about thirty yards behind it. They were connected with each other by a well-constructed, covered way made of fascines. They were also hard at work all day in the summer-house to the east of the fort, within fifty yards of the gun tower. This increased activity was probably due to the news of the near approach of Colonel Kelly's force from Mastuj, and to the hope of taking the fort by a last desperate assault before it arrived.

That night there was an unusual quiet. It almost seemed as if the enemy had left their *sungars*. But early in the morning of the 7th a terrific fire was opened upon the walls. The enemy advanced with wild outcries, and were evidently in great strength. In an instant everyone was at his post, and steady volleys were poured into the darkness on the garden side of the fort, the direction whence the chief attack seemed to be coming, and the inlying picquet were posted near the main gate ready for any emergency that might arise. In this, as in all other attacks, the difficulty was to decide against which portion of the fort the main attack was directed.

Suddenly a strong light was seen near the gun tower. A fire platform to illuminate the walls at night had recently been erected, and it was at first thought that one of these fires had been lit by mistake; but

Gurdon, who was in charge of that part of the fort which contains the gun tower, sent down word that it had been fired by the enemy, by placing lighted faggots against the wall, which, being made almost as much of wood as of stone, readily took fire. Mr. Robertson, with the Punialis, and what may be termed the odds and ends of the garrison, horse-keepers and servants, at once went off to endeavour to extinguish it. Everyone else remained quietly at his place, for the firing of the gun tower might have been only a feint to divert attention from an attack on the waterway. But as this did not seem to be the case, the inlying picquet was soon afterwards sent by Townshend to carry up water and earth in their greatcoats.

In the tower itself an exciting scene was going on. From the *machicoulis* galleries to the south and east, men tried hard to subdue the flames with earth and buckets of water. Inside the darkness was very great; outside the flames raged fiercely, whilst constant volleys from the enemy, only thirty yards away behind the walls of the summerhouse, made a rattle and roar that must have been deafening. Several men fell down, blinded with splinters from the woodwork. All worked their hardest; Kashmiri servants, throwing aside their natural timidity, vied with each other in bringing water and earth, and stood the racket of the bullets with wonderful pluck. An old tracker from Gilgit, a servant of Captain Townshend, worked hard in the eastern gallery until wounded in two places. It should be mentioned that the *machicoulis* galleries could only hold one man at a time, and, when one was wounded, another had to be substituted.

A brave little Gurkha sat in the south gallery, ladling down water on the bonfire beneath, calmly replacing the protecting shutters as they were knocked over by the bullets, and then ladling away again, until he, too, was badly hurt, and had to be dragged out of his perilous post. For an instant there was a panic, no one caring to replace the wounded man, and then Bidrina, the same Gurkha officer who had helped to bring in Captain Baird, stepped out into the gallery and worked there until he too was exhausted and had to be pulled inside. By that time, however, the fire at the foot of the tower had been got under. Unhappily, the walls were now thoroughly alight on the outside; so great holes had to be knocked through the lower stories of the tower, through which the flames could be attacked. These holes were most dangerous places.

At one of them the British agent was hit; so too were several of the men, amongst them being Captain Campbell's orderly, a non-com-

GURKHA SEPOY 4TH KASHMIR RIFLES AND
MAHOMMEDAN SERVANT.

missioned officer of the Central Indian Horse, Duffadar Mahomed, who died of his wounds a day or two after. To add to the difficulties of the besieged, a strong wind just then sprang up from the south, and no sooner were the flames got under temporary control, than a gust of wind fanned them into fresh life. But by ten o'clock the fire was altogether subdued, and the enemy driven off. Not content with carnal weapons, they had with them a number of *mullahs*, or priests, who, sheltered behind a wall, prayed incessantly for the fall of the tower and the success of the attack. By half-past ten all was quiet again in the tower, and officers and men were able to take a little rest and sleep. I am told that the striking thing about the attack was the admirable way in which the Puniali men and the non-combatants, such as officers' servants, water-carriers, *syces*, and even the Chitralis who were inside the fort, helped the *sepoys* in their dangerous work.

CHAPTER 8

Flight of the Besiegers on the 18th April

Townshend now took very careful precautions to prevent a similar attempt being made to fire any of the other towers. He had earth and buckets of water stored in the basements and upper stories of each tower, and along the parapets. The *bheesties* or water-carriers were made to sleep in front of the hospital with full *mussacks*, as the leather water bags which they carry are called, mounds of earth were placed in the courtyard, and large holes were dug in the ground there as reservoirs for water. He also arranged a special fire picquet of Punialis. That these precautions were not unnecessary was very soon shown, for on the evening of the 15th, the enemy again tried to fire the gun tower, but were repulsed without difficulty. Mr. Robertson's wound was a bad one, but he refused to lie up, and went about as usual, for he was afraid that it might dishearten the men if they saw that another of the officers was incapacitated.

The following night, April 16th, the enemy made a determined attack in force upon all sides of the fort simultaneously, but were driven back with much loss. During the day large bodies of men had been noticed going in the direction of Mastuj, and several dead bodies were seen being carried in. This showed that there had been a fight in that direction, and that many men of position had been killed, for they would not have taken the trouble to bring back the bodies of those of inferior rank.

The enemy now began to make a great noise with drums and pipes in Nizam-ul-Mulk's summer-house, keeping it up continuously for several days. Rab Nawaz Khan, the news writer, who was so badly wounded on the 3rd March, but who was by this time nearly recovered, suggested that this might possibly be done to drown the noise of mining, an art in which the Pathans are great adepts, Umra Khan having taken several forts by that means. Men were therefore put on to listen, and at midnight the sentry in the gun tower reported that he heard the noise of picks.

About eleven o'clock the next morning, the sound of mining was distinctly audible, and within a few feet of the tower. It was evident that there was no time to be lost, and that a sortie must be made at once to blow up the mine. Harley and a hundred men were told off for this duty. It was decided to wait until the afternoon, and about four o'clock Harley and his men came out of the fort at the garden gate, and rushed straight at the summer-house. It was held by about forty Jandolis, who promptly fired a volley which killed two of their assailants, and then fled; but not before some sharp hand-to-hand fighting had taken place. The head of the mine was found to be in the summer-house, and the mine itself to be full of Chitralis. Harley stationed his men in the summer-house, and with five *sepoys* jumped down himself into the mine.

The Chitralis, about thirty in number, came swarming out, and a fierce fight ensued. They were rapidly bayoneted and the mine cleared, and the bags of gunpowder placed in position and tamped. Harley was trying to light the fuse, when two Chitralis who had lain quiet till then at the end of the mine tried to make their escape. In the struggle that followed one of the *sepoys* fired, and must have hit one of the bags, for immediately there was a violent explosion, and the mine was blown up from end to end. Harley was knocked over by the concussion, and the Sikhs who were with him had their hair and their clothes singed, but were not otherwise hurt. All this time the *sepoys* in the summer-house had been subjected to an extremely heavy fusillade from the Jandolis, who, retreating quickly towards the river along the side of the garden wall, quickly threw up fascine breastworks, from behind which they kept up a steady fire, and from all the loopholed walls of the garden a constant fire was also maintained.

The enemy seemed to think that the garrison were making a final and desperate sally, so not only from the walls about the fort, but from the *bazaar*, and from the village of Danin across the river as well, a heavy fire was directed both against the fort and against the summer-house. Having finished their work Harley and his men, whose dash and gallantry had carried all before them, hurried back to the fort, having been out of it an hour and twenty minutes. Of the hundred

MOUTH OF THE MINE, AND GARDEN WALL, ALONG WHICH
THE JANUOLIS RETREATED—RIVER IN THE DISTANCE.

who went out twenty-two were hit—nine mortally.

A curious instance of devotion was noticed during the sortie. One of the regimental *bheesties* ran out with the *sepoys*, and was struck almost at once by a bullet in the jaw. He was hurried back to the hospital, where his wound was dressed, and as soon, as the bandages had been put on he rushed out again, and had to be forcibly brought back and detained. This caused him the greatest possible distress, and he kept saying that the *sepoys* must be in want of water, and complaining that he was not allowed to go to them. Thirty-five of the enemy were bayoneted in and around the summer-house, and about a dozen more were shot near it. The dead and dying as seen from the gun tower presented a ghastly spectacle, until night closed the scene, and they were carried away by their friends. But even after the siege was raised the summer-house still bore gruesome traces of the stubborn fight that had taken place there.

In the evening a couple of countermines were begun by the garrison underneath the gun tower, with the object of making a circular mine to intercept the enemy's mine should they try to make another. It was necessary to be on the alert, for a report had reached Mr. Robertson that the Jandolis had sworn to take the gun tower, and that they would not rest until they had done so. The sentries were therefore ordered to listen attentively, and to at once report any suspicious noises they might hear. During the night one of the native clerks came to Captain Townshend and said, "Sir, I hear the voice of knocking," and at first it certainly sounded like the noise of another mine being made, but on careful investigation it was found that it was not.

By a strange chance the knowledge that the mine was being made, and that it was so close up to the walls, was known in Simla almost as soon as it was to the garrison. A letter written by one of the Jandolis was captured by the *Khan* of Dir's men on the 14th April. In it the writer said that a mine had been begun, and had already been advanced to within a few yards of the tower, and that they intended "to blow up the tower with gun cotton." It was this information that caused Sir Robert Low to order General Gatacre to push on to Chitral as rapidly as possible, and he had actually got as far as Dir when the news reached him that Colonel Kelly's force had arrived in Chitral, and that the siege had been raised.

A curious feature was noticed in connection with the mine, showing how skilful the Jandolis are in work of that kind. All engineers know how difficult it is to mine straight; but this mine, though it was

Demolished summer-house with lower part of the gun tower in the background.

quite fifty yards in length, and had two turns in it, after the final turn headed in a perfectly straight line for the foot of the tower. It was very shallow, only eighteen inches below the ground, and the direction was most likely preserved by sticks driven through the surface at short intervals to serve as guides.

On the 18th the enemy were very quiet, and the garrison worked hard all day at the countermines. But in the middle of the night a man came and stood outside the fort, calling out that he had important information. He proved to be Rooshun, a brother of Fateh-Ali-Shah, who had been of such use to the garrison in getting them grain before the siege began, and who was inside the fort. He called out that Sher Afzul had fled, and that the relieving force was near at hand, so early the next morning, April 19th, Gurdon was sent out to reconnoitre. He found the political officer's house deserted and no one in sight anywhere. The scene inside the fort when the relief was announced was exceedingly dramatic.

The English officers shook hands with the little *mehtar*, and the Chitralis in the fort crowded round calling out "*Mubarik—mubarik*"— "Victory—victory"; and the Bengali clerk said to one of the officers in a voice broken with emotion, "Sir, I am born again, and if I live for twenty years more I shall never forget this time." Poor man,—he had had a terrible experience. He was not a fighting man, nor of a fighting race, and it is little wonder that he was rejoiced. His way of expressing himself was somewhat comical, but none of the officers of the garrison will have him laughed at, for they say that he never once flinched or shirked his work, although he had a man killed by his side while he was serving out stores, but that all through the siege he did his duty manfully and well.

About three o'clock in the afternoon of the following day, the 20th, Colonel Kelly arrived from Mastuj with the 32nd Pioneers, No. 1 Kashmir Mountain Battery, and some native levies from Hunza and Nagar; and a day or two later the British agent heard from Major Deane, the political officer with Sir Robert Low's force, that Sher Afzul and a number of Chitralis had surrendered and were prisoners at Dir.

So ended a very memorable siege. It had lasted altogether forty-six days, and there had been thirty-nine men killed and sixty-two wounded. The *sepoys* had suffered greatly from want of food, as to eat horseflesh like the officers would have been against their creed, and the "*ghi*" had long run out. They had only had half-rations of flour, and when the relief came they were weak and emaciated from want of food and sleep; but their endurance and pluck were most admirable. The Sikhs especially showed extraordinary nerve. The worse the outlook the cheerier they grew. They would sit all day cleaning their rifles, with a quiet smile as though the anticipation of defeat had never entered their minds. They felt sure, they said, that the Government would not desert them, and that in due time help would come.

As one of them tersely put it, "*Sircar ka hath astr hai, lekin bahut lumbar.*" "The arm of the Government is slow, but it reaches very far." Indeed no praise can be too great for the Sikhs, who were the very, backbone of the defence. They not only endured hardship and privation without a murmur, but they fought with a quiet, dignified courage that in itself inspired confidence.

On April 21st the British agent issued the following farewell order to his escort:—

Consequent on the retreat of the Jandol Khan and Sher Afzul on the night of the 18th, and the near approach of Colonel Kelly with the Gilgit force, the siege of Chitral came to an end. The British agent's escort now comes under the command of Colonel Kelly, commanding the Gilgit force. In bidding good-bye to the troops who so gallantly held the Chitral Fort against overwhelming numbers and under unprecedented conditions, the British agent desires to place on record his appreciation of the admirable manner with which all ranks fought and worked, and cheerfully endured terrible hardships. Their bravery and fortitude were beyond all praise, while their discipline remained unimpaired. The soldiers of the Queen-Empress and those of H.H. the *Maharajah* of Kashmir fought side by side with splendid devotion and with admirable comradeship, and the British agent will ever remember with gratitude and heartfelt emotion their heroic valour and resolution. It will be his duty, and his very great pleasure, to bring their unique services to the notice of His Excellency the Viceroy, and to His Excellency the Commander-in-Chief in India. Captain Baird, the brave General Baj Singh, and Major Bhikam by their noble behaviour, and their heroic death at the beginning of the hostilities, set an example which all ranks have shown themselves worthy of emulating.

CHAPTER 9

Defence of Reshun

Soon after the British agent and his escort had proceeded to Chitral Captain Ross and Lieutenant Jones, with two companies of the 14th Sikhs, moved up from Gilgit to Mastuj.

Between Mastuj and Gilgit there are only two fortified posts, one at Gupis at the head of the Yasin valley, and the other at Ghizar, fifteen miles on the Gilgit side of the Shandur Pass, which lies between it and Mastuj. Last year, (as at time of first publication), a strong fort was built at Gupis, as it is necessary to hold in check from there the men of Tongir and Darel. But at Ghizar there is only a native house with a few outbuildings, and it would be a very hard place to defend. Lieutenant Gough of the Gurkhas, who was on special service with the Kashmir Imperial Service troops, was left in command at Gupis with a garrison of 140 Kashmir Rifles, and Captain de Vismes with 100 rifles at Ghizar.

Between Mastuj and Chitral, a distance of sixty-six miles, there is no fort, only a small fortified post at Buni, eighteen miles from Mastuj. The fort at Mastuj is very old and dilapidated, and unfit for defence, but it is in a better position and much less commanded from the neighbouring hillsides than the fort at Chitral. The Yarkun River, which is afterwards known as the Chitral or Kunar River, flows past it from the north through a valley which ultimately terminates in the Baroghil Pass. Another valley joins it at right angles to the east and leads to the Shandur Pass, over which the road to Gilgit passes. There is a more direct road than this to Ghizar, but the Pass over which it goes is more than 16,000 feet in height, and exceedingly difficult.

On the 16th January Lieutenant Fowler, R.E., was ordered to proceed from Gilgit to Gupis with twenty Bengal sappers and miners. He remained there about a fortnight, when he was directed to go on to

Chitral with Lieutenant Edwardes of the 2nd Bombay Grenadiers, but who, like most of the officers in Gilgit, was on special service with the Kashmir troops. They had a terribly cold march over the Shandur Pass, but succeeded in reaching Mastuj in eight days.

There they found the political officer, Lieutenant Moberley, D.S.O., in command, Ross and Jones having gone out a day or two before to apprehend one of the petty local chiefs who had been breaking down the road and stopping the mails. On the 5th March they left Mastuj with seven days' rations, meeting Jones on the way, bringing back the Rajah and a few of his followers prisoners. They reached Buni the same evening, and found Captain Ross there; and also a *subadar* of the 4th Kashmir Rifles who had been sent ahead with forty men and sixty-eight boxes of ammunition.

The next morning Ross returned to Mastuj, and Edwardes and Fowler continued their march, taking the Kashmir Rifles and the ammunition along with them. About three o'clock in the afternoon they arrived at Reshun, where they were told that there was a hostile gathering a mile or two ahead. There had been continual vague rumours going about during the past few months, and, as they had had no information from Chitral that any trouble was impending, they were at first inclined to discredit the story. Their suspicions were, however, awakened by the fact that for some days there had been no letters from Chitral; and they thought it well to be on the safe side, and to take every precaution in case they should meet with opposition. They therefore chose a defensible position near the river, and made a *sungar* or breastwork there with the men's kits and the ammunition.

The next morning, leaving the bulk of the *sepoys* on guard, they took a few men and proceeded to reconnoitre before going further. They first carefully examined all the hills and cliffs with a telescope, and as they could see no signs of an enemy, Edwardes, who was in command, sent Fowler on with eight or nine sappers and some timber to mend the road, which was reported to have been broken down. Immediately after leaving Reshun it goes a thousand feet straight up the side of an exceedingly steep hill, and down an equally steep descent on the other side. There it comes out on a small open plateau, where Edwardes halted, and Fowler went ahead to mend the road, which winds through a defile along the face of a precipitous cliff overhanging the river bed. Directly opposite is the mouth of the Ovirgh Nullah, which ends in a broad fan on which stands the village of Parpish, terminating abruptly in a cliff over 100 feet in height.

When Fowler got into this defile he was fired upon, not only from the village on the opposite side of the stream, but from the cliffs above, from which the enemy also rolled down rocks upon him, a very favourite method of attack in Chitrali warfare. He therefore rejoined Edwardes, who had also come under fire. One of the *sepoys*, a *naik*, was mortally wounded, and several other men were hit, so that it was necessary to retreat at once, as the enemy were in greatly superior numbers.

This, however, was a difficult operation, as between them and Reshun was the steep hill over which they had come, and which was quite bare and exposed to the enemy's fire. Fowler's *syce* had brought up his pony, and he put the wounded *naik* upon it and succeeded in bringing him in, but he died soon after. Fowler had himself been hit by a bullet, which caught him sideways in the back, but which fortunately only inflicted a flesh wound.

As they neared Reshun another body of men appeared on the hills above the village, and with their previous assailants closed in round the breast-work, which though conveniently placed for obtaining water was commanded both from front and rear from about 500 yards. In a very short time eight men were killed and fourteen wounded,, and it was evident that they could remain no longer in so exposed a position. They therefore occupied a cluster of houses a few hundred yards distant, turning the enemy out with the bayonet, and hastily making it as defensible as they were able. The means they employed for this purpose are best described in the words of their official report. In that they say:

The sappers, under fire, proceeded with the work of making *sungars* on the roof, loopholing walls, blocking up entrances, and making communications and interior arrangements. We had every reason to expect an attempt would be made to rush us during the night, probably before dawn, as, being the *Ramzan*, the enemy would cook in the evening.

The materials available for making *sungars* were the mud bricks of which the houses were built, roof timbers, boxes, and other timbers lying about. Before dusk we started to get in the ammunition and wounded. This was done by volunteers from the Kashmir *sepoys*, who, for 100 yards between the *sungar* and the *bagh* ran the gauntlet of a heavy fire, but none of them were hit. Already dead-tired these men behaved splendidly. At sunset the fire slackened, and the whole of the ammunition was in soon afterwards, also a few ration-bags and kit-bags. Then every man was posted and told to strengthen his cover for himself. This they did very cleverly, but it must be remembered that we were in expectation of a rush any moment, that the men had had a hard day, no food and little water.

All night there was desultory firing, and the men had no time to have any food. They had to stand to their posts, ready for an assault. The cold too was very trying, the ground being covered with snow. All the next day the firing continued, but no serious attack was made, and they were able twice to sally out and fill all their vessels with water.

The village stands on a little plateau in a confined valley encircled by hills. Below it the Yarkun River has worn out a deep, narrow gorge with a precipitous cliff on the village side about 150 feet in height. From the hills behind the village several little streams run down towards the river, which are directed into the irrigation channels by means of which all cultivation in Chitral has to be carried on.

The first thing the besiegers did was to divert these rivulets from their channels, and the besieged soon found themselves in a sore plight for water. The brink of the cliff was nearly a quarter of a mile away, and when it was reached there were only one or two places where a difficult track led down to the water's edge. A stone wall ran along the top of the cliff, behind which the enemy ensconced themselves, and they also occupied a house standing between the cliff and the block of houses seized by the besieged. To obtain water was therefore a very perilous task. Every evening under the cover of the darkness a party was sent out with large water vessels, each carried on a pole by two *sepoys*, a different path being chosen each time in order to mislead the enemy.

On the night of the 9th a determined assault was made. The enemy were repulsed with much loss, but five of the Kashmir Rifles were killed and six wounded, a very serious loss to a garrison already reduced to less than fifty men, and surrounded by an enemy who could not have been less than a thousand, and who more probably numbered over fifteen hundred.

The following night, March 10th, Fowler made a sortie with twenty men to get water. They crept quietly up to a bend of the wall on the cliff where they could not be seen, and surprised forty or fifty of the enemy sitting beside a large fire—the glare of which prevented them seeing clearly—and charging suddenly, killed more than twenty of them. While they were out the village was assaulted, but Edwardes succeeded in repelling the attack before they returned.

Fortunately the garrison had no lack of food. They had taken seven days' rations with them from Mastuj, and they found fowls and eggs and flour in the village, but they suffered greatly from want of water, though they eked out their scanty supply by collecting rain water in their waterproof sheets. They also tried to dig a well, but after going down twelve feet they came upon rock, and had to give it up.

After the assault on the 10th the enemy contented themselves with investing the village, and getting gradually closer up to it. This they had no difficulty in doing, for there was plenty of cover—stone walls, and detached houses and trees—of which they could avail themselves. Only about thirty yards off was a large *chunar* or sycamore tree in which they built a crow's nest from which they kept up a very galling fire. They were able indeed to get so close up to the walls without exposing themselves, that several times they tried to knock holes in them with battering rams, and the weak places had in consequence to be loopholed and barricaded from the inside.

The village is built in blocks, the houses in each block communicating with each other; and in one of them, in accordance with their creed, were burnt the bodies of the Hindu *sepoys* who were killed, those of the Mahommedans being buried. Another of the houses they converted into a hospital, and though neither of them had any knowledge of surgery, they did what they could for the men who were wounded, but that was not much as they had no proper appliances. They could only make rough splints and crutches. Edwardes, too, had a little carbolic acid and some carbolic tooth powder, which they made into a lotion, and dressed the wounds with that.

The houses in Chitral are low, only eight or ten feet in height, and have flat roofs. The rooms are dirty and very dark, and open into a court-yard, which is generally full of all kinds of rubbish. Between the houses are narrow paths often not more than three feet in width—just enough to allow a man to pass. The enemy, after many unsuccessful attempts, finally succeeded in establishing themselves in a house just alongside the block of houses held by the besieged, and tried hard to drive a hole through the wall.

But though they were at such close-quarters—not more than five feet off—they were not able to do much damage, for the walls were

HOUSE HELD BY EDWARDES AND FOWLER AT RUSHUN

of stone and too thick for a bullet to come through, and the garrison maintained so watchful a scrutiny from a breastwork they had built on the top of their own roof, that the enemy did not dare to venture up on theirs—the few who did so being shot at once.

CHAPTER 10

Capture of Reshun by Treachery

On the 13th the enemy hoisted a white flag, and a Pathan came forward and asked for a parley. Jemadar Lai Khan, one of the Bengal Sappers and Miners, was sent to speak to him. He said he was Ghulam Said, a Jemadar of Umra Khan, and that he had formerly been in one of the Baluch regiments. He stated that Mahomed Isa Khan, a foster-brother of Sher Afzul, had come up from Chitral to stop the fighting, and it was arranged that Mahomed Isa Khan should have a conference with Edwardes. When he came he said there had been fighting in Chitral, but that peace had been made, and he offered the garrison a safe conduct either to Mastuj or Chitral. Edwardes concluded an armistice for three days, and wrote to the British agent in Chitral, and also to Mastuj. The terms of the truce were faithfully observed; the garrison being allowed to fetch water unmolested, and sheep, fowls, and eggs, being supplied to them.

On the 14th, Edwardes had a second interview with Mahomed Isa Khan, who was accompanied by Yad Gar Beg, another of the Chitrali *adamzadas*, or nobles, and who confirmed what Mahomed Isa Khan had said the day before. On the 15th the snow had melted, and Mahomed Isa Khan asked if they might play a game of polo, and as they would be under fire all the time, his request was granted. Indeed, it is difficult to see how it could have been refused without bringing the truce to an end.

Mahomed Isa Khan then asked the officers to come out and have tea, and join in the general rejoicing for the restoration of peace. This proposal was anxiously considered, and under the circumstances it was thought advisable to go. The wall of the polo ground was only sixty yards away, and there was a gap in it, at which the interviews with Mahomed Isa Khan had always taken place, so that they were covered all

74

the time by the rifles of their own men. They asked that the tea might be served there, and a bed was placed in the gap, on which Yad Gar Beg and the officers sat, Mahomed Isa taking part in the game. After it was over permission was asked for a dance, which it is always the custom in Chitral to have after a polo match, the losing team having to do the dancing.

The snow in melting had left a wet place on the ground in front of the bed, which was shifted a few feet to one side to a drier bit of ground. It was difficult to take objection to this, for though it brought them away from the gap, and behind the wall, it was only three feet in height, and they were still under the cover of their men's rifles, and the Chitralis who were sitting on the polo ground on the further side of the gap, were all full under fire, so that it seemed impossible that treachery could be contemplated.

After the dance was over a number of their men came over to the wall and the officers stood up and said they would go in. Mahomed Isa, who was sitting between them, immediately threw an arm round each of them, and the men who were nearest him seized them and dragged them along under the wall. A heavy fire was at once opened by the garrison, and many men were killed. The Chitralis then attacked the house and took it by assault, putting most of the defenders to the sword, two of the Sikhs, it is said, shooting themselves to avoid capture. The officers were stripped of nearly all their clothes, and were tightly bound hand and foot.

A day or two later they were taken on to Chitral, which they reached on the 19th March. There they found Jemadar Lai Khan and eleven other *sepoys*, who had been taken prisoners after the assault, and who had been sent on to Chitral ahead of them. They were unbound and taken to see Sher Afzul and Majid Khan, Umra Khan's representative. Both expressed their great regret for the treachery that had been practised upon them. An armistice had just been concluded with the fort, and the commissariat clerk was allowed to bring them clothes and blankets. Before that they had suffered much from the cold, having been deprived of their boots and socks, and from the tightness of their bonds.

Jemadar Lai Khan and the other *sepoys* had been brought on from Reshun by a more direct road than that along which Edwardes and Fowler were taken. His account gives a very vivid idea of the difficulty and danger of these hill roads. He said:

The road beyond Reshun had been cut. In one place the planks over which the road is carried had been cut away, and a man could only cross with bare feet, in parts a man with boots could not pass.

They were kept in Chitral till the 24th, when the truce came to an end, and were then marched down to Umra Khan at Drosh. He received them politely, and treated them well, and finally told them that if they liked he would send them back to the British agent in Chitral fort. They asked if they might take their *sepoys* with them, but he said "No," so they declined to go back by themselves. Umra Khan told Edwardes to write to the British agent that he intended to keep him shut up in Chitral fort until he chose to accept his escort down to Peshawur.

The next day, the 26th, they started for Jandol, and arrived at Barwar on the 30th, after a very rapid and fatiguing march. The officers were given ponies and the best food that could be obtained, and were treated with much kindness and consideration both on the march and afterwards in Jandol.

They were always strongly guarded, and were allowed to communicate with no one except through Umra Khan, but they believe that these precautions were taken mainly for their protection, for had they not been strictly guarded, they might have been killed at any moment by some fanatic.

Umra Khan himself treated them with the greatest courtesy. Twice he took them out hawking with him, and always insisted that his men should treat them respectfully. He gave Edwardes back his sword, which had been taken at Reshun, and sent to him by Mahomed Isa as a present, and he tried unsuccessfully to get Fowler's back for him also. Finally he sent them both back with an escort unharmed into Sir Robert Low's camp at Sado, and they do not believe that he ever intended that any injury should be done to them. The *sepoys* were also set free, and allowed to make their way back as best they could.

Jemadar Lai Khan found his way to Peshawur across the almost unknown territory of the Mohmunds. The account he gives of his journey is interesting.

There was a man named Mihrban Shah, a servant of Umra Khan, who used to be in the sappers, and who deserted from Peshawur many years ago. He recognised me, and told me the *khan* would look after me. He took me to his home, and kept me there two days. I felt that I did not know the country or the roads; but I induced two men, friends of Mihrban Shah, to help me. They saw me on my way to Nawagai. I went as a beggar, barefoot, bareheaded, and nearly naked. At Nawagai they left me. There I fell in with a '*talib*' (religious student) who was going to the war. I entreated him to give me a book, saying that I was a man of Yusufzai. and wanted to return home. He gave me a book to carry, which helped me to pass off as a *talib*. This book saved my life in several places. I spent three days on the hills on the way to Peshawur.

On the fourth day I reached Shabkada; a *sepoy* of the border police gave me food and bedding, and so I came on to Peshawur. At a pass above the district I was stopped and beaten and searched, but allowed to go alive. I had been warned not to travel by the regular routes or tracks as they were stopped by bands of men. The Mohmunds have been stopping all travellers on routes through their hills. I came by a short foot-track not passable for mules or animals.

Two of the other *sepoys* made their way across the hills from Jandol to the Chitral Relief Force, rejoined their regiment, the Bengal Sappers and Miners, under Major Aylmer, V.C., and accompanied it over the Lowarai Pass to Chitral, and finally went back to Gilgit with a detachment under the command of Fowler, Edwardes following a day or two later with Colonel Kelly and the Pioneers.

They had to pass through Reshun, and it must have been with a strange feeling of emotion that they visited again the place where they had suffered so terribly, and where they had made so gallant a stand against hopeless odds. They owe a deep debt of gratitude to Umra Khan for his magnanimous forbearance—a forbearance so rarely shown by the Pathans to the conquered that it has created in India a feeling not only of astonishment, but of respect.

It has been stated that the Government have decided to withdraw the troops from that part of the Barawal Valley between Janbatai and Chutiatan, and also from Jandol; and that the *Khan* of Dir will administer the Barawal Valley, while Bajour is to remain under tribal government. It is to be hoped that this is an indication that in course of time Umra Khan is to be restored to Jandol.

CHAPTER 11

The Disaster at Karagh

When Edwardes and Fowler found that they were likely to meet with opposition in Reshun they sent back word to Mastuj, and Captain Ross started at once to their assistance with Lieutenant Jones and ninety-three men of the 14th Sikhs. He left thirty-three men in the post at Buni, and went on with the other sixty towards Reshun. Midway between the two places is a village called Karagh, and half a mile further on the road enters a narrow defile where the river twists through precipitous cliffs.

They had advanced nearly to the end of this defile when they were suddenly fired upon from a *sungar* on the opposite bank, and almost at the same moment a large body of men appeared on the rocks above them, and began hurling stones down upon them. The enemy were seen to be in great strength, so Ross decided that it would be better to retire to Karagh where they could seize and occupy a house until relieved, than to try and force their way through to Reshun. He therefore ordered Jones to hurry back and hold the Karagh end of the defile with ten men in order to cover their retreat.

Jones endeavoured to do this, but in the meantime the enemy had closed in behind them, and he found himself confronted by a *sungar* built right across the path. From this *sungar* so heavy a fire was opened upon him that only two out of his ten men remained unwounded. So he rejoined Ross, who had collected the rest of the men in a cave just underneath the road. Fortunately the river was low, and the mouth of the cave was accessible. A little later, when the river rose with the melting of the snow, it was entirely under water.

After an anxious consultation they determined when it became dark to make another attempt to fight their way out of the defile; and about eight o'clock they rushed out in the hope that the enemy would be off their guard; but they found them waiting for them, and not only came under a galling fire, but were in great peril from the stone shoots of which several had to be crossed.

These stone shoots are terrible places. They are formed by the mountain side breaking almost sheer away, and are just not precipitous enough to prevent the loose stones from remaining in a state of suspension, but the inclination is nevertheless so steep that the least movement amongst the stones is sufficient to put them all into motion, and an avalanche of boulders comes rushing down the shoot like a waterfall. How dangerous they are may be judged from the fact that the natives will not attempt to cross them if sheep or goats are moving about on the cliffs above, for if the stones are once set going they descend with such frightful rapidity that there is no possibility of escape.

The enemy had stationed themselves on the tops of the shoots, and the whole party were in danger of being annihilated. They therefore returned to the cave, and waited till the moon rose when they again sallied out, and tried to climb up the face of the cliff immediately above them; but before going very far they were stopped by a precipice, and had to go back once more to the cave. There they remained without food during the whole of the following day; and when night came they felt that they must try and cut their way out under cover of darkness, no matter what it might cost them, rather than wait in the cave to be starved. So in the middle of the night, about 2 a.m., when they thought the enemy would be least likely to be on the alert, they made a sudden attack on the *sungars*, and after a desperate struggle succeeded in taking them; but in doing so Ross was shot in the head and killed on the spot.

The enemy, who had only retired a short distance up the hill, kept up an incessant fire, and so did the men from the other side of the river; and when at last they reached the end of the defile they had very few men left. Just before getting to the *sungars* they had to cross a bad stone shoot, and so terrible an avalanche of stones was poured down upon them that not many reached the other side. Two months afterwards I was shown the place, and was told that the bodies of at least thirteen men, and probably of a good many more, lie buried underneath the *débris* lying between the footpath and the river. It is impossible to get at them, for any attempt to do so would again bring down the whole quivering hillside, and end in frightful disaster.

What happened afterwards is best told in Jones's own words. In his

THE KARAGH DEFILE.

report, he says:

> I and seventeen rank and file reached the *maidan* on the Karaeh side of the hill in safety. When I got there I halted, and reformed my men, and stayed there some ten minutes, keeping up a heavy fire on the *sungars* on both sides of the river in order to help any more of the men who might get through. While we were halted here two bodies of the enemy's swordsmen attempted to charge us, but were checked by volleys, losing heavily. As the enemy now showed signs of cutting our line of retreat, I considered it was time to retire, especially as two more of my party were killed, and one mortally wounded, while I had been waiting there. Of the remainder I myself and nine *sepoys* were wounded. We retired slowly on Buni, where we arrived about 6 a.m. It was quite impossible to bring away any wounded men who were unable to walk with us. It was equally impossible to bring their rifles, and therefore a certain number of these, about forty, fell into the enemy's hands.

It was afterwards found that about thirty men who had been wounded, or who had been finable to get past the stone shoot, re-treated again to the cave, where they were hemmed in by the enemy on all sides. They were able to get water, but they had no food, and gradually got weaker and weaker. But in spite of hunger and wounds they held out for more than a week, and then only surrendered under a promise that their lives should be spared. This promise, like most Oriental promises given under similar conditions, was not kept. One or two men were taken possession of by the more far-seeing of their captors, who afterwards obtained a reward for sending them back to Colonel Kelly's force; but the rest were mercilessly put to the sword, and, if the native reports may be believed, in the most cruel possible way.

At Buni Jones found the native officer and the thirty-three men who had been left there. He did not think it prudent to try and push through to Mastuj, as he was told that the enemy were collected in force at Nisa Gol, the place where Colonel Kelly afterwards defeated them. He therefore put the post into as good a position for defence as he could, and waited for the attack which he expected every hour would be made. Strange to say, the enemy never came near them, probably hoping that troops would be sent to their assistance, and that they might be able to cut them all off together.

Lieutenant Moberley arrived on the 17th, exactly a week after, with a hundred and fifty of the Kashmir Rifles, and fifty of the Puniali levies, and they marched back with him to Mastuj, where Captain Bretherton had been left with only sixty Kashmir Rifles. It was fortunate that the enemy did not attack the fort while Moberley was away. Had they done so, Bretherton would have had great difficulty in defending it with such a handful of men.

Immediately after Moberley's return they closed in round it, and invested it closely, building *sungars* on the surrounding hills, and keeping up a constant desultory fire. But they never attacked in earnest, and seem to have intended to starve the garrison out, as no doubt they would have done if Colonel Kelly's force had been delayed for any great length of time. So little indeed was its arrival expected by them, that when they hurriedly evacuated Mastuj a letter was found in one of the houses they had vacated, urging them to invest the fort strictly and reduce it by starvation, for no troops would be able to get over the Shandur Pass for some time to come. They were about fifteen hundred in number, and were under the command of Mahomed Isa Khan, who had come up from Reshun after his treacherous capture of Edwardes and Fowler.

Why they did not attack Jones at Buni is quite inexplicable. Probably they expected that he would try and get to Mastuj, and meant to attack him somewhere on the march where they could take him at a disadvantage. Of the sixty men who started from Karagh, Ross and forty-six men were killed, and of the remaining fourteen, Jones and nine others were wounded. The marvel is that any of them escaped.

CHAPTER 12

Colonel Kelly's March

Captain Bretherton sent off a letter from Mastuj on March 18th, which reached Gilgit on the 21st, giving details of the disaster at Karagh; and from Gilgit the information was telegraphed to Simla. The Government had already decided that an expedition should be sent through Swat and Bajour to relieve Chitral, and on receipt of this bad news they pushed forward their preparations with the utmost dispatch, so that it should start not later than April 1st.

Chitral was believed to be about a hundred and eighty miles from the base of operations at Nowshera, and it was hoped that a flying column, taking with them rations for twenty days only, and marching without tents and as light as possible, might be able to reach it in eighteen days. But the country this column would have to traverse was practically unknown. The information with regard to it was of the vaguest and scantiest character, and it was impossible to foresee the difficulties that might be encountered.

It was anticipated that the fanatical tribes of Swat and Dir would offer an obstinate resistance, and it was known that there were several formidable rivers to be crossed, and one, if not two, snowbound mountain passes. Any one of these obstacles might cause unavoidable delay, and the loss of even a day might prove fatal to the garrison of Chitral, who could not but be hard put to it, for it was known that they were only rationed up to the end of April.

It was impossible to send relief from India through Gilgit and Yasin, as lofty passes intervene, which are not open, except for three or four months in the summer. There are two routes to Gilgit: one through Kashmir and Astor, the other by Abbotabad and Chilas, through the Kagan valley, and up the Indus to Bunji. The route through Chilas is much the shorter of the two, but it is not that generally in use, because

COLONEL KELLY, (CENTRE) WITH THE 32ND PIONEER OFFICERS

the bulk of the troops in the Gilgit agency are Kashmir Imperial Service troops, and the commissariat base by the Astor road is not in India proper, but in the Kashmir valley, from which almost all the supplies are drawn.

The question of commissariat and transport is indeed an all-important one, for the country that is traversed by both routes, and, indeed, the whole of the Gilgit district, is a sterile wilderness of mountains, on whose bleak, precipitous sides nothing will grow; so that all the food, not only for the troops, but for the transport animals also, has to be brought up from Kashmir in the few months during which the passes are open.

The Burzil Pass, which is 13,800 feet in height, lies between Kashmir and Astor, and on the Chilas road the Babusar Pass is almost equally lofty and difficult. Moreover, neither of these passes is open until the middle of June, so no troops could be sent through to Gilgit until then. Fortunately the 32nd Pioneers, under Colonel Kelly, were there already. They had their headquarters at Bunji, and were engaged in making the road to Chilas. Bunji is on the Indus, at the point where the roads from Astor and Chilas meet, and is only thirty-eight miles from Gilgit.

An order was therefore telegraphed to Colonel Kelly on March 21st to march at once, and as rapidly as possible, to Chitral. He left Bunji the same afternoon, and started from Gilgit with an advance party on the morning of the 23rd, the rear-guard having to wait for No. 1 Kashmir Mountain Battery, which arrived from Nomal that afternoon, and following the day after. The advance party consisted of two hundred of the 32nd Pioneers under Captain Borradaile, Lieutenant Bethune the adjutant, Lieutenant Cobbe, and Surgeon-Captain Browning-Smith; and the rear-guard of two hundred more men of the 32nd Pioneers, under Lieutenant Peterson and Lieutenant Cooke, two guns of No. 1 Kashmir Mountain Battery, and a hundred men levied from Hunza-Nagar and Punial, under the command of Akbar Khan, the *Rajah* of Punial, and Wazir Humayun, the Prime Minister of Hunza, both very fine specimens of native warriors.

Wazir Humayun is the man of whom the following graphic description is given in *Where Three Empires Meet*:

Safdar Ali, it will be remembered, succeeded to the throne after murdering his father; he then proceeded to expel the Wazir Humayun from the country, and appropriated his wife. The two

Hunza–Nagar levies

boys remained with their mother, while Humayun fled to Chitral and became a firm ally of ours. He is described as a man possessed of many excellent qualities. It was known that he had many friends in Hunza, and that a large party in that country was ready to follow him.

As such a man would be of service to us, he had been recalled from Chitral by our Resident; and his two boys, hearing of this, had left Safdar Ali and their mother to rejoin their father. The little lads appeared very glad to see us, realising that they had now got safely out of the tyrant's clutches. It is somewhat strange that he let them go. In one of his fits of rage he might have murdered them to revenge himself on their father, whom he hated; or he might have kept them with him as hostages. At the time I write this the exiled Humayun is once more in possession of his estates, and is Wazir of Hunza; while Safdar Ali, who had so wronged him, is a friendless wanderer on the wastes of Turkestan.

From Gilgit the road winds forty-six miles along the course of the Yasin River to Gakuch, the chief village of the little tributary state of Punial. Habibulla Khan, the son of Afyat Khan, the Rajah of Gakuch, and a number of Punialis, accompanied the British agent to Chitral, and did excellent service all through the siege.

Before the Hunza men left Gilgit they had a war dance, which Mrs. Bretherton, the only English lady in Gilgit, told me was a very weird performance. There is a vivid description of Hunza dancing in *Where Three Empires Meet,* so I will not describe it again now. A goat was tethered by the side of the ring, and as one of the dancers drew near to it, with a sudden stroke of his *tulwar* he whipped its head off amid the wild cries of the bystanders. The scene must have been one not easily to be forgotten, with the light of the torches and of the moon falling on the excited barbaric figures and on the majestic background of snow-clad mountains.

On the other side of the river, opposite Gakuch,. is the mouth of the Ishkoman valley, which leads up over the Khorabort Pass to the little Pamir Steppe. The Pass is only three days' march from Gakuch, but it is lofty and difficult, and not much used, most of the traffic coming over the Darkot Pass at the head of the Yasin Nullah.

Gupis is twenty-four miles beyond Gakuch, over an excellent road all the way. It is not like the beautiful ten-foot road from Gilgit to

Kashmir, which is a really wonderful bit of work both in engineering and construction, but it is a good hill road. After Gupis it degenerates into a mere track, going up and down a succession of steep hills and across the face of some exceedingly awkward "*paris.*" In one or two places it is very bad indeed. A couple of miles before Gupis a mountain torrent comes rushing down into the Yasin River through a narrow gorge which leads to one of the passes into the country of the Darelis and Tongiris. Fifteen miles on the other side of the fort the Batresghur Nullah leads up to another pass, and the road to a third pass comes down close to Ghizar.

The Darelis and Tongiris are a collection of turbulent, unsettled tribes upon whose movements a constant watch has to be maintained, so Colonel Kelly was obliged to leave a sufficient number of men to garrison Bunji and Gilgit, and to hold Gupis and Ghizar against a possible incursion not only from Darel and Tongir, but from Chilas.

The fort at Gupis was built by the Kashmir troops under Townshend and Stewart only last year, and has strong stone walls and a well-built covered waterway. It is of course exposed to fire from *sungars* on the surrounding hills; in these narrow valleys it is impossible to find a site which is not; but the water supply is safe, and if garrisoned with a mere handful of men it would be hard for an enemy not provided with guns to take it.

It stands at the entrance of two valleys. One, through which the Yasin River flows, going up to Ghizar, and terminating at the Shandur Pass; the other, on the opposite side of the river, leading up to Wakhan, over the Darkot and Baroghil Passes. Neither of these passes is difficult for travellers, and a fair amount of traffic passes over them from Samarkand and Bokhara. I asked one of the natives how far it was from Gupis to Bokhara, and he said it could be done in thirty-seven easy marches. I should mention that if the valley of the Yarkun or Kashkar River, which is also known lower down in its course as the Chitral or Kunar River, be followed up beyond Mastuj, it, too, will be found to terminate in the Darkot Pass, immediately behind which is the Baroghil.

When the advance party reached Ghizar, where they found Captain de Vismes, the Gilgit settlement officer in charge, it had been snowing hard for five days. It was impossible to get on, so they waited for the rearguard to come up, which it did on the following day. It had been joined at Gupis by Lieutenant Stewart, R.A., who took charge of the guns, by Lieutenant Oldham, R.E., with forty Kashmir Sappers,

No.1 Kashmir Mountain Battery

and by Lieutenant Gough with 100 Kashmir Rifles.

On April 1st, in spite of the snow, the whole column started for the Shandur Pass. When they had gone about three miles, it was found that a number of the Yasin villagers, who had been impressed to carry the baggage, had run away during the night. Stewart galloped off to try and find them, and coming up with about thirty compelled them to return with him to the force, which however they did not reach until late in the afternoon. He had a very long, tiring ride, and his pony dropped in the snow with exhaustion, and had to be abandoned.

When the column had gone about four miles the battery mules stuck hopelessly in the snow. After doing all they could to get them along, it was found that in two hours they had only gone a few hundred yards, and it was evidently useless to try to advance until the weather cleared a little. Part of the force therefore returned to Ghizar, where they could obtain food and shelter; but Borrodaile was left at a hamlet called Teru to make another attempt. He had with him 200 of the Pioneers, Oldham and his forty sappers, Wazir Humayun with the Hunza levies, all the coolie transport belonging to the force, and rations for ten days.

Heavy snow fell all the next day, and it was impossible to move. It was bitterly cold, and the men, who had no tents and only their greatcoats, suffered terribly. Colonel Kelly, however, sent Stewart and Gough on from Ghizar with the guns, and after a very severe march they managed to get through to Teru. The guns could not possibly have been brought along if Gough's Kashmir Rifles had not volunteered to carry them, asking permission to do so through their native officers.

The following morning, April 3rd, the whole of Borrodaile's party started for Langar at the foot of the pass, the guns being partly carried by the men and partly dragged on sledges. Langar is only five miles from Teru, but they did not get there till eleven at night, the snow was so deep. It is a bare plateau 9,000 feet in height, at the foot of the ascent to the pass, which is 12,400 feet in height. There was no shelter there of any kind; not even rocks behind which the men could shelter themselves from the bitterly cold wind. They had to stay out all night on the open snow, crowding round wretchedly small fires, for there was scarcely any firewood to be had.

Early the next morning Borrodaile and the Pioneers started with Oldham and his sappers and the Hunza levies to try and get over the pass. Stewart and the guns had to be left behind, for it was hopeless to move them until a path of some kind had been trodden through the snow. Borradaile, with great difficulty, managed to struggle across to Laspur on the other side of the pass, where he entrenched himself, and waited for the rest of the force to come up. His achievement was a very fine one. Had the enemy occupied the pass they might have given great trouble, and indeed might have stopped the force from getting across at all, for it would have been very difficult to make use of the guns in the deep snow. But they never dreamt that the troops would attempt to cross in such severe weather, and were quite taken by surprise.

There is a gradual ascent of 3,000 feet up to the pass from Langar, the pass itself being a level plain rather over five miles in length, over which the wind has full room to gather strength. It is shut in by mountains 15,000 or 16,000 feet in height, and has a large lake in the middle. This lake was of course frozen over and covered with snow, and was undistinguishable from the rest of the plain. At the end of the pass there is an easy descent to the village of Laspur, which is about the same height as Langar, but not nearly so exposed and bleak, there being no houses or cultivation of any kind at Langar.

Stewart and Gough came over with the guns on the following day, the men again partly carrying them and partly bringing them along on sledges. The majority of the *sepoys* had blue spectacles, but many had not. They tied their *pugarees* over their eyes and over their ears, but they suffered dreadfully from snow-blindness and from frostbite. There were thirty cases of snow-blindness and twenty-six of frostbite in the advance party alone, and when the whole force had got over it was found that there were altogether sixty-eight cases of snow-blindness and forty-three of frostbite. The men had with them only 15 lb. kits. They carried greatcoats and eighty rounds of ammunition, and wore *poshteens* or rough sheepskin coats. But for the latter they would have suffered much more severely. On the 6th April, Colonel Kelly and Lieutenant Beynon came across to Laspur with the remaining fifty of the levies, leaving the rest of the Pioneers to follow as soon as possible.

Borrodaile and Stewart were sent that afternoon to reconnoitre towards Gasht, the guns being carried by *coolies*.

On the 7th there was a halt to collect supplies, and on the 8th the force started for Gasht, which was reached that evening without opposition, but a reconnoitring party brought back word that the enemy, under Mahomed Rafi, were immediately ahead. So the next morn-

91

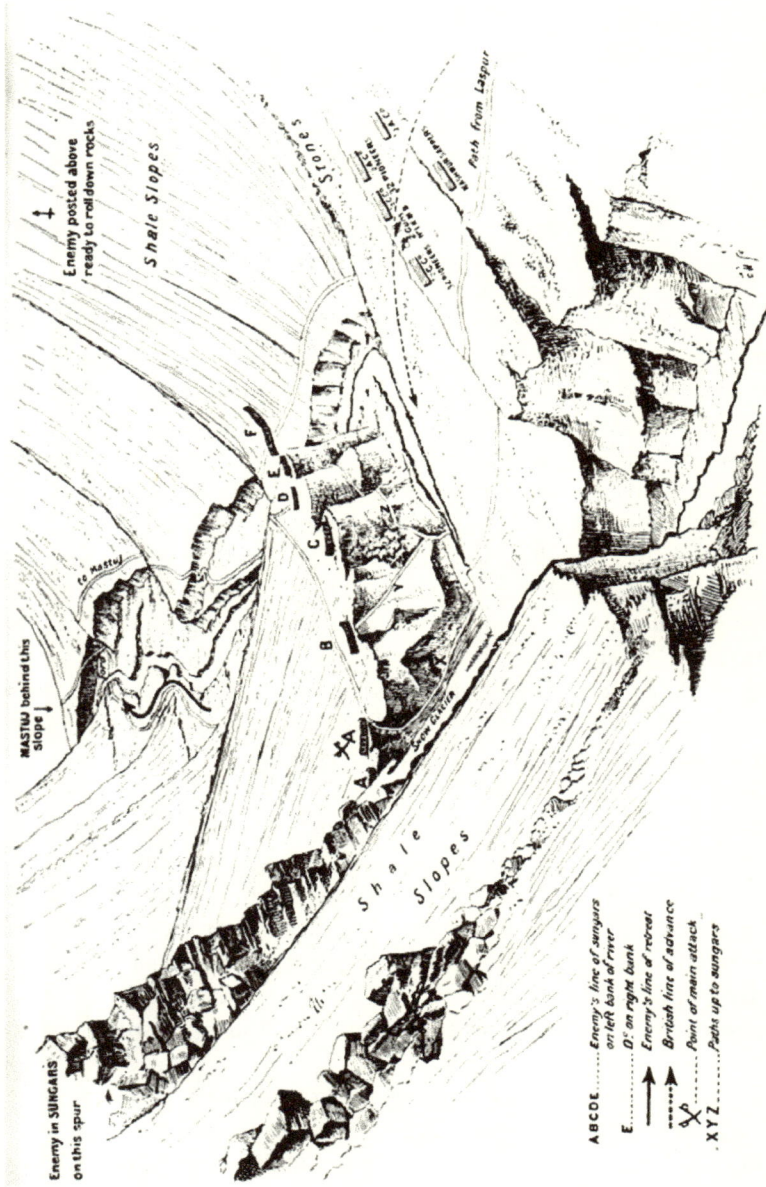

Enemy in SUNGARS
on this spur

MASTUJ behind this
slope

to mastuj

Enemy posted above
ready to roll down rocks

Shale Slopes

Shale Slopes

Stones

Stones

Shale
Slopes

Path from Laspur

ABCDE ...... *Enemy's line of sungars*
on left bank of river

E. ——→ *D': on right bank*

——→ *Enemy's line of retreat*

•••••→ *British line of advance*

✗ *Point of main attack*

X Y Z *Paths up to sungars*

PLAN OF THE ACTION AT CHAKLEWAT

ing Beynon was sent with fifty levies up the hills to the left, and the Hunza men, under Wazir Humayun up those to the right, the rest of the force proceeding slowly along the road down the valley.

About eleven o'clock Beynon's party were seen on the hillside flanking the enemy, and the guns opened on the enemy's *sungars*, who were unable to face the shells and fell back hurriedly to another line of *sungars*, a little to the rear. The guns were advanced and again brought to bear upon them, when they fled precipitately, leaving twenty-five killed and fifty wounded. Colonel Kelly's force having five men wounded, but none killed. In his telegraphic despatch, dated the 10th April, Colonel Kelly says:—

I marched to Gasht on the 8th, with 200 Pioneers, 40 Kashmir Sappers, 2 guns, 1 Kashmir Mountain Battery, and 50 Hunza levies. The guns were carried by *coolies*. On arrival in camp, on proceeding to a hill in front, I saw the enemy at work on *sungars*, three miles ahead at Chaklewat, called Darband in the map. Lieutenant Beynon, on going forward to higher hills with a few Hunza levies, discovered that they had constructed several *sungars* on the left bank of the river. He immediately sent back for Raja Akbar Khan, with 50 Punial levies.

On the morning of the 9th instant, I sent the Hunza levies on a high hill on the left bank of the river, to work towards the rear of the *sungars*, and the Punial levies on the hills to the right to turn out the men prepared to roll stones down should we proceed by the right bank of the river. I advanced with the remainder of the force to drive the enemy out of their position. The bridge being broken was repaired, and we crossed to the right bank. The guns were carried through the river. Ascending on to the opposite line of the *sungars* on the left bank of the river, I directed the attack on the first *sungar*, a covering party of Hunza levies on the left bank having already come into contact with a small party on the hills.

The enemy held No. 1 *sungar* till the rifle and gun fire commenced, and then they gradually fled by twos and threes, and eventually evacuated No. 1 *sungar*. The fire was then directed on No. 2 *sungar*, and the infantry moved down the cliff to the river, and ascended by steep paths to No. 1 and 2 *sungars*, fording the river. On arriving on the left bank of the river, the enemy fled from all the *sungars*, including those in the hills on the right bank prepared for throwing down stones. The action lasted one hour.

The position was of unusual natural strength, and the disposition of the *sungars* displayed considerable tactical ability, they being placed on the edge of the high cliffs of the left bank of the river commanding the road, the right bank for over a mile being devoid of cover. Their object was to compel us to take the road on the right bank, and expose ourselves to their fire from the left bank, and stone shoots on the right. The enemy are computed at from 400 to 500 men, armed with Martinis and Sniders. Five dead were found in the *sungars*, and all the ground covered by the action has not yet been searched. Their wounded were not found, so presumably they were carried off. The enemy fled towards Mastuj as rapidly as possible. Our casualties were, one *sepoy* of the 32nd Pioneers severely wounded, one *subadar* and two *sepoys* of Kashmir Sappers slightly wounded.

We continued to advance to Mastuj by the left bank till within one mile, when we forded the river, and crossed to the right bank. We arrived at 5 p.m.; the baggage arrived at 8 p.m. The Mastuj garrison was found well. The garrison noticed at about 1 p.m. that the enemy who were investing the place were gradually vacating their position, and by evening all had gone towards Chitral, enabling them to turn out after eighteen days' investment. On April 10th, Captain Bretherton started to return across the Shandur. Lieutenant Jones and the wounded of the 14th Sikhs are doing well. The former received a bullet wound in the right biceps, and severe contusion by a rock on the right elbow. I am forwarding his report. Two hundred Pioneers are expected tomorrow. The Lashpur Valley is now clear.

The two hundred Pioneers duly arrived the day after, and on the 12th Beynon made a reconnaissance down the road to Chitral, and found that the enemy had taken up a strong position at Nisa Gol, about a mile to the north of the village of Sanoghar, so the whole of the troops advanced against them on the following morning, April 13th, the guns being mounted on country ponies, Lieutenant Moberley with 100 Kashmir Rifles accompanying them.

Mastuj Fort stands on a plateau in the angle formed by the meeting of the Yarkun River and the stream that comes down from the Shandur Pass. The road crosses the Yarkun River by a rude cantilever bridge and ascends the cliffs on the opposite side. After a steady rise for some miles it comes out upon a wide elevated plateau about four miles in length. On the left is the deep precipitous gorge formed by the Yarkun River, while snow-capped hills rise abruptly from it on the right. About a third of the way across the plateau there is a deep rift, 250 feet in depth, and not more than 200 yards across. This has been made by a mountain stream which, coming down a very steep ravine in the hills above, has rent its way through the loosely compacted conglomerate of which the plateau is composed. The sides of the cleft are of exactly the same height, and until it is reached no break to the continuity of the plain can be perceived. The enemy had *sungars* all along the opposite edge of the cleft, and also on the hillsides above.

The Puniali levies were sent up the hill on the right to get above the ravine and come down on the other side on the enemy's flank, and the rest of the force advanced to about 250 yards from the enemy's *sungars*, upon which the guns opened fire. There was no cover of any kind on the plain, so they came full under the fire from the *sungars*.

The enemy's position was so strong that if they had stuck to it doggedly they must have inflicted terrible damage before they could have been dislodged, but they could not stand the artillery fire, to which they are not accustomed; it seemed to demoralise them altogether, and after their *sungars* had been shelled for some little time they left them and fled across the plain to their rear, losing a good many men as they ran from the volleys poured in upon them by the Pioneers. In all probability they would have made a more determined resistance had they not seen the levies descending the hill and about to take them in flank.

Almost at the same time Oldham, who with his sappers had been let down the cliff with rope ladders, and who had found a path leading up the cliff on the other side, made his appearance on the top quite close to their *sungars*. They were afraid then of being caught between two fires, and fled without attempting any further stand. Colonel Kelly in his despatch gives some interesting details of the fight:—

After the first *sungar* had been somewhat silenced, Lieutenant Beynon, my Staff Officer, informed me that a goat path had been observed on the other side of the *nullah* and a practicable spot to attempt a crossing, and asked me for leave to take the Kashmir Sappers to make a practicable path down into the *nullah*, and the company of the 4th Kashmir Infantry to cross it,

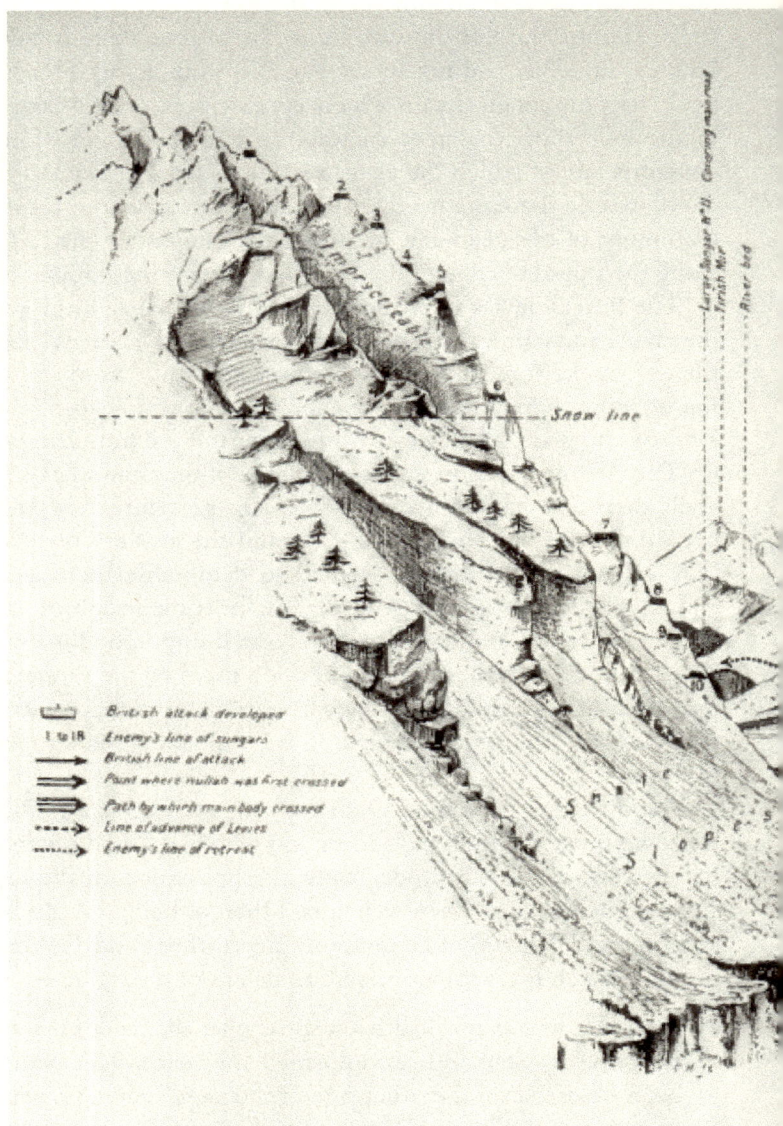

Snow line

British attack developed
1 to 18   Enemy's line of sungars
           British line of attack
           Point where nullah was first crossed
           Path by which main body crossed
           Line of advance of Levies
           Enemy's line of retreat

PLAN OF ACTION

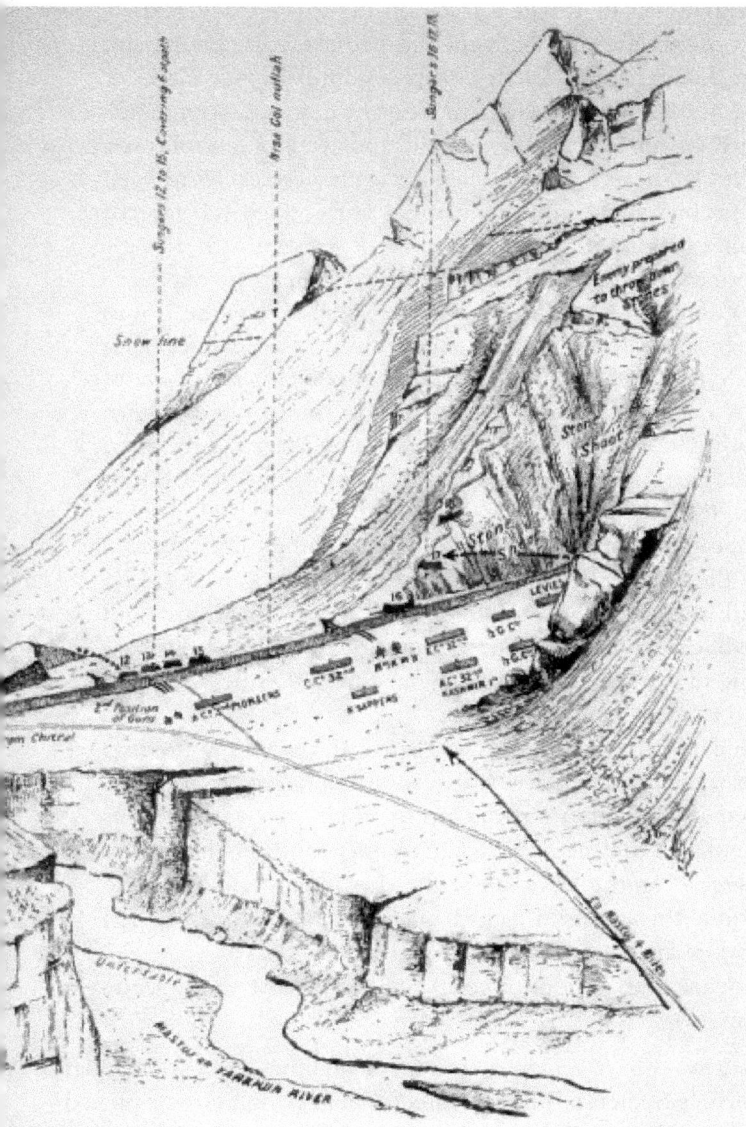

Snipers 12 to 16, Covering Sepois

Nisa Gol nullah

Snipers 16 N.

Snow line

Enemy prepared to throw down stones

Stone Shoot

Stone Sp

LEVEL

2nd Position of Guns

12 13 14 15

A C.   PIONEERS

C.C. 32ND

R★M★X

C.C. 32ND

6 G.C.

A.C. 32ND KASHMIR I★

6 G.C.

6 SAPPERS

Churral

UNFORDABLE

MASTUJ or YARKHUN RIVER

T Nisa Gol

when made, under cover of the fire of the deployed infantry. The scaling ladders were brought up and lowered, and after half an hour's work a track was made to the bottom of the *nullah* and an ascent by the goat track on the further side assured. A party of ten Kashmir Sappers and Miners, with Lieutenant Beynon, Lieutenant Moberley, commanding the 4th Kashmir Infantry, and Lieutenant Oldham, Royal Engineers, commanding the Kashmir Sappers, descended, and were being followed by the 9th Kashmir Infantry, when some gun-cotton lying open on the ground at the commencement of the track was ignited by a bullet striking it.

A temporary retirement of the line of those near the explosive to cover some thirty yards in rear was ordered, but the troops were speedily brought to the front again when no danger of an explosion was to be apprehended. Eventually a party of about fifteen reached the other bank, and almost simultaneously with the turning movement of the levies, who had reached the large *sungar* and its vicinity, having run the gauntlet of a stone-shoot in their course.

The appearance of these bodies on the enemy's left caused a general flight, and they streamed out of their *sungars* in a long line, with the guns firing at ranges from 950 to 1,425 yards and under volleys from the infantry. The ground falling away near their line of retreat did not favour our fire, and protected them till almost out of range.

A general advance was then made across the *nullah* by the two paths previously mentioned, and as soon as a company could be mustered, it was sent in pursuit; but the flight of the enemy was very rapid, and they came no longer under our fire. The enemy in the *sungars* on the left bank of the river disappeared into the snow, while those on our right bank who escaped our fire fled towards Drasan.

We bivouacked that night opposite Sanoghar, close to the scene of action.

Some curious old *Korans* were found lying about, and I was shown one of the Bible Society's Bibles, printed in Persian, which was picked up in one of the houses. The enemy were commanded by Mahomed Isa Khan, and were estimated to have been about 1,500 in number. They left fifty dead on the field, and were seen carrying a great many dead and wounded over the plain before their assailants could get across the fissure. Colonel Kelly's force had eight men killed and sixteen wounded; the battery suffering the heaviest loss.

The diagrams both of Chaklewat and Nisa Gol have been kindly drawn for me by Lieutenant Beynon. They show, more clearly than a verbal description can, the great natural strength of the enemy's positions and how skilful were the dispositions made by Colonel Kelly for attacking them. The natives look upon Nisa Gol, not without reason, as one of the strongest defensible positions in the whole of Chitral, and' it cowed them altogether, and took all the spirit out of them for further resistance, to find that Colonel Kelly with a greatly inferior force was able alter a few hours' fight to turn them out of it with so much loss to them and so little to himself.

It is not to be wondered at that they look upon him with the greatest admiration as a commander. An interesting fact in connection with Nisa Gol is that it seems probable that it is the same place as the "Nysa," which Curtius mentions as being the last place to which Alexander the Great advanced in his reconnaissance up the Khoes, the ancient name of the Yarkun River. He says that "Nysa" was at an elevation of about ten thousand feet; and Nisa Gol must be at very nearly the same height. Alexander thought the country beyond impracticable, so he retreated back to Chitral, and advanced eastwards from there through Yagistan.

The next day, April 14th, it was found that the road in front had been cut, so a long march of over twenty miles was made over the tops of the hills to Kila Drasan. The fort there was found to be empty, and the village deserted. The manoeuvre proved a very successful one. The enemy had expected that the force would take the same route through Karagh that Ross had taken, and were completely discomfited by this unexpected detour.

At Drasan, Phula, a *sepoy* of the Kashmir Rifles came into camp, dressed like a Chitrali. He had been helped by a villager to make his escape after the treacherous capture of Reshun, and had been in hiding ever since. He said that between 2,000 and 3,000 men had fled up the Murikho valley after the defeat at Nisa Gol, and that Mahomed Isa had gone on to Chitral with only fifty or sixty men. The bridge over the river at Drasan was found to be broken down. It was patched up sufficiently for the men to cross, the animals having to swim. Khusht was reached the following night, after a long trying march in pouring rain.

The day after the march was continued to Lun, and the following day to Barnas. This last was a short but very fatiguing march, which took ten hours to do. The road was broken down in several places, and so much delay was caused that the camp was not reached until past nine o'clock, when it was quite dark. The river, which was in flood, had to be forded close to the camp. It was about four feet deep and very cold, and the men could only get over by going across in batches of ten or twelve at a time, and holding each other up. Many of the baggage *coolies* must have been swept away and drowned had it not been for the ready resource and pluck of the levies. They formed up in a line just below the ford, and whenever a *coolie* was washed off his feet they waited till the stream carried him down to them, and catching hold of his pack, which floated on the surface, swung him round by it on to his feet, and pulled him ashore.

The levies did splendid work throughout. They could go up the steepest and worst bits of ground without even pausing to take breath, and at Nisa Gol they scaled an almost precipitous stone shoot to attack one of the enemy's *sungars*. It was found that there were only rations left for two and a half days, so a short march was made the next day to Moroi, and foraging parties were sent out who brought back enough for another day. The villagers said that Mahomed Isa had slept there the night before. On the 19th the march was continued to Kogazai, a large village about thirteen miles from Chitral.

From information given by the villagers there it was anticipated that the enemy would make a last stand at Gulen Gol, but on reaching that place the *sungars* were found to be empty, and no resistance was met with anywhere. At Kogazai Colonel Kelly received a letter from the British agent telling him that the siege had been raised, and that Sher Afzul had fled.

The following afternoon, April 20th, the force entered Chitral. Colonel Kelly had achieved a really magnificent feat of arms. His force had marched 350 miles in thirty-five days, over exceedingly difficult country and in the face of an enemy. The passage of the Shandur Pass was in itself so splendid a performance that it has thrown all the other incidents of the march into the shade; but all the marches were difficult and arduous. The greatness of the achievement may be estimated by comparing it with the passage of the Balkans by Gourko, and with the passages which have been made from time to time of the Alps. The distances in these marches have never exceeded seventy-five miles, and the highest altitude attained has been under 7,000 feet. The passage of the Balkans only took thirty hours, and that it was not nearly so trying while it lasted, the following extracts from the *Daily News* correspondence will show.

A few days ago two battalions of the Prasbrajensky regiment began to work on the path, graded it somewhat, widened it nearly the whole extent, and cut steps in the ice in the steepest place up to the summit. A portion of the way was in full sight of the Turkish redoubts, east of Araba-Konak. Therefore work could be undertaken only at night, and when the advance was made the path was so good that it was believed that cannon could be brought up with horses. . . .

When the twilight came on we all started down the mountain, everybody on foot, for the path was so steep and slippery that no horse could carry a rider down. A snowstorm began before we had gone far, and doubled the difficulty of the descent. Part of the way we slid down like so many schoolboys, and afterwards let ourselves down through the undergrowth, for the road was one solid sheet of ice. Two or three miles of this work brought us to the head of the valley, and we were over the Balkans, breathless with the exertion of the descent. We paused a moment, and shook hands in the darkness, and then pushed on to the village, where we slept under a roof as peacefully as if the Turk, were twenty miles instead of one mile away. How the cannon came down this side it is impossible to tell, for the road was for a long distance only a gully made by the rain, and the incline was so steep and slippery that it was almost impossible to stand upon the road. However, the four-pounders were in the village at daybreak, and the regiment of the line filed through in the forenoon.

What made the Shandur Pass so hard to cross was the time of year in which the crossing was effected. During the winter, when the snow is hard, it is not nearly so bad; but in the spring, when the snow is melting, it is a very difficult matter. The snow clogged and gripped the men's feet so that they could scarcely lift them; and if they went in the slightest off the little beaten track made by the advance party, they plunged in up to their waists, and, owing to the difficulty of transport, a very small quantity of supplies could be taken. Each *sepoy* carried two days rations for himself, and only rations were brought sufficient for seven days more. After they were exhausted the force had to de-

NATIVE OFFICERS

BALTI COOLIE.

pend upon what supplies could be obtained from the country through which it had to pass, and in Chitral, at the best of times, there is very little to be had. The *sepoys'* rations consisted of a pound and a half of flour, and a very little *"ghi,"* or clarified butter. They had nothing else, except when they were able to get a little millet, which the Chitralis grind and make into cakes. It is not unpalatable, but there is not much nourishment in it.

The cold in the pass in the melting snow was exceedingly great, and one or two days there was heavy rain which tried the men greatly, as they had no tents; and it is wonderful that they stood the exposure so well upon so meagre a diet.

It is true there were forty-three cases of frostbite, but none of them proved fatal; whereas in the passage of the Balkans, which lasted a much shorter time, there were seventy-nine men frozen to death.

The difficulties of transport and commissariat in the Gilgit agency are always very great, but during the hostilities they were intensified a hundredfold. The pack animals could not get through the snow, so Bretherton organised a corps of Baltistan *coolies*, who did excellent work.

Directly after Colonel Kelly arrived at Mastuj, Bretherton hurried back to Ghizar, collected a number of the villagers, and, with them and some of his own *coolies*, cut a track through the snow, two feet wide and three feet deep, right across the Shandur Pass for more than five miles. It was done in three days, and on April 21st the transport animals were bringing over supplies to Mastuj, and thence right on to Chitral.

Bretherton had exceedingly difficult work, necessitating great anxiety and exposure, for he had charge of the whole of the commissariat and transport arrangements between Gilgit and Chitral, and had to cross the Shandur Pass no less than three times. When Ross left Mastuj for Reshun, he wrote an urgent letter to Ghizar, ordering him to come over to Mastuj by forced marches. This he did, reaching Mastuj on March 10th with 100 Kashmir Rifles. His arrival was most opportune, for if he had not been in the fort, Moberley would not have been able to go down to Buni to bring back Jones and the survivors from the disaster at Karagh.

To add to his anxieties there were constant rumours that the Darelis and Tongiris were coming down. If they had done so, his difficulties would have been greatly augmented; for it would have been impossible to have protected the whole of the straggling line of Balti *coolies*.

COLONEL KELLY, CAPTAIN BORRODAILE, AND OFFICERS OF THE 32ND PIONEERS

They might easily have done it, had they known, when almost all the troops in the Gilgit agency were on the other side of the Shandur Pass. They would only have had to reckon with De Vismes and 100 men at Ghizar, and Gough and 140 men at Gupis. Fortunately they remained quiet, but if the fort at Chitral had fallen, or if Colonel Kelly's force had met with any serious reverse, they would almost certainly have attacked, not only Ghizar and Gupis, but Gilgit and Bunji also.

MAXIM GUNS ON THE MARCH

CHAPTER 13

Advance from Mardan

Early in March, as soon as the Government of India saw that war was inevitable, the First Army Corps consisting of 14,000 men, was ordered to be mobilised at Nowshera and Hoti Mardan. Major-General Sir R. Low, K.C.B., in command of the Oudh District, who had seen much service in the Mutiny, in Afghanistan, and in Burma, was appointed to command the expedition. Brigadier-General Bindon Blood, C.B., R.E., being the chief of the staff, and Lieut.-Colonel J. H. S. Craigie, of the Highland Light Infantry, the Assistant Adjutant-General. The three brigades were commanded by Brigadier-General A. A. Kinloch, Brigadier-General H. S. Waterfield, and Brigadier-General W. F. Gatacre, D.S.O., the line of communications being under Brigadier-General A. J. Hammond, V.C, A.D.C., C.B., D.S.O., with Major A. F. Barrow, C.M.G., of the 12th Bengal Infantry as base commandant, and Brevet-Major S. C. H. Munro, Seaforth Highlanders, as Deputy Assistant Adjutant and Quartermaster-General. Major Deane, the Deputy Commissioner of Peshawur accompanying the force as chief political officer.

At first it was not intended that the troops should move across the border until the 5th April, but news was received on the 22nd March of the disaster at Karagh, and that the garrison at Chitral were in serious danger, and it was deemed necessary to move without delay. The main difficulty was to get the commissariat and transport for so large a body of men ready in time, but Lieut.-Colonel A. V. Yaldwyn, who was in charge of the commissariat, and Major Fitzgerald, who was in charge of the transport, were equal to the emergency. By working day and night, on the morning of the 1st April the troops were able to move forward, the 1st Brigade to Lundkhwar, and the 2nd and 3rd to Jellala, all marching without tents, and taking with them supplies for twenty days only. The next morning the 2nd and 3rd Brigades went on to Dargai, which is a village about four miles from the foot of the Malakand Pass, the line of communication troops being left at Jellala.

The weather was cold and wet, and the rain made the roads soft, causing a good deal of delay. It had been given out that the 1st Brigade were to attack the Shahkot Pass; but this was only a ruse in order to divide the enemy, and keep them from concentrating on the Malakand, which was the real object of attack. Captain Turner, commandant of the Viceroy's Body Guard, the intelligence officer of the 1st Brigade, subsequently explored the Shahkot Pass, and found it to be much more difficult than the Malakand and more strongly fortified, General Low's feint in that direction was a fine piece of strategy, and in all probability caused a number of the enemy to collect there who would otherwise have been on the Malakand Pass.

In the middle of the night orders were accordingly sent to the 1st Brigade to proceed at once to Dargai, in order to support the 2nd Brigade in an attack on the Malakand. Early on the morning of the 3rd, a reconnaissance was made by General Blood and Major Deane, and large bodies of men were seen to be collected on the sides of the pass, waving banners and dressed in white, the usual war-garb of the Mahommedan fanatic. It was evident that the tribes meant to dispute the passage in earnest, and about 7 o'clock the 2nd Brigade were ordered to proceed towards it from Dargai. Sir Robert Low in his despatch gives the following account of what followed:—

I learnt on the 1st of April that all three passes into Swat, *viz.*, the Malakand, Shahkot, and Morah passes, were held by the enemy, and the majority of them occupied the Shahkot and Morah passes. At that time the disposition of the troops of this force was so arranged as to attack the Malakand and Shahkot passes simultaneously on the morning of the 3rd of April. The 1st Brigade was then at Lundkhwar, on the road to the Shahkot pass; the 2nd and 3rd Brigades were at Jellala, on the road to the Malakand pass. Consequent on the above information I determined to deceive the enemy as to my intention, by advancing the cavalry to Pali, on the Shahkot road, on the 2nd of April. The idea that that pass would certainly be attacked was maintained, but I directed the 1st Brigade to join me at Dargai, opposite the Malakand Pass, on the morning of the 2nd of April, and hoped by a forced march on the night of the 1st of April to reach Dargai by 8 a.m. and carry the pass on the 2nd of April with the three brigades.

A storm of wind and rain, however, raged all through the night of the 1st, and at midnight I was obliged to abandon my intention of a night march, it being an impossibility for the men to load the transport in such darkness, rain, and wind. All that could be done, therefore, was to start at daybreak and collect the three brigades at Dargai on the 2nd, and make the attack on the 3rd of April. I may note here that, so far as deceiving the enemy as to my intention of attacking only one pass, the plan was completely successful, though the attack took place a day later than I had hoped, for the enemy had not sufficient time to get across the hills and help their comrades on the Malakand Pass between the evening of the 2nd of April, when they must have fathomed the plan, and the morning of the 3rd.

The attack took place on the morning of the 3rd with the 2nd and 1st Brigades. It was my intention to use the 2nd Brigade only, the 1st being in rear with its mule transport, ready to cross the pass as soon as it was captured, and march on the Swat River; but, as will be seen, I found the pass so strongly held and so obstinately defended that to gain the victory I had to utilise both brigades, and at the final moment I had only one regiment in reserve, the other three regiments of the 1st Brigade, as well as all four regiments of the 2nd Brigade, being engaged in the attack.

Starting from Dargai the pass at first goes through a gradually narrowing valley to the north for about two miles; then bends to the north-east for a mile and a half, where the high hills on the west drop precipitately into the pass. On reaching the bend of the pass to the north-east it was apparent that the pass was strongly held on the west side, the whole range being lined by men with flags and banners. At this point the 4th Sikhs were sent to occupy a spur which jutted out from the range to the west, and they had to remain there covering the advance for the day.

The Guides Infantry were directed to ascend the highest point of the western hill, and after gaining the summit to turn along the crest and enfilade the position of the enemy, which evidently extended from the highest point to the end of the range, and where, as already noted, the hill precipitately descends into

SEPOYS GUARDING PRISONERS AFTER THE ATTACK OF THE MALAKAND PASS

the pass. The Guides Infantry had a most arduous task to perform. They had to ascend the highest peak of the range, about 1,500 feet high, and attack and capture several *sungars* full of the enemy, which were held by riflemen and crowds throwing rocks and stones down; and their advance was necessarily gradual. Meanwhile, as the force advanced, the position of the enemy was disclosed. They occupied the whole of the crest of the western hill, with numerous *sungars* down the sides of the hill, each commanding the one below it, and their main strength was on the northern end of the hill, where it precipitately descended into the valley.

The hills on the eastern side of the pass were not held by the enemy till after the point where the western hill dropped into the valley. Full advantage was taken of this fact. There were three mountain batteries with the troops in action—namely, Nos. 3 and 8 Mountain Batteries, Royal Artillery, and No. 4 (Derajat) Mountain Battery of four guns, in all sixteen guns; and these took up position after position on the eastern slope of the valley, and most successfully prevented any concentration of the enemy. When the infantry advance was ordered, it soon became apparent that if the assault was delayed till the position was turned by the Guides, that the action would be unduly delayed, and the Guides themselves seriously outnumbered.

At this time I also ascertained that although the pass appeared to lie in the valley itself, and to round the corner of the western hill, where it dropped into the valley, yet that beyond this point there was no path or roadway whatever, the valley being blocked with huge blocks and boulders, and that the crossing of the pass lay to the left, over the heights to our left which were so strongly held by the enemy.

Action was at once, therefore, taken to carry the hill to the left, which from this point was about 1,000 feet high. The Gordon Highlanders were directed up the crest of the western hill from the point where it touched the valley; the King's Own Scottish Borderers were directed up the centre spur; the 60th Rifles were directed up the slopes from further back in the line; while the Bedfordshire Regiment and the 37th Dogras pushed on and rounded the point from which the Gordon Highlanders commenced the ascent, and turning to the left ascended the hill from the northern side, the 15th Sikhs being held in reserve.

MACHINE GUN DETACHMENT,
KING'S OWN SCOTTISH BORDERERS

MACHINE GUN DETACHMENT, DEVONSHIRE REGIMENT

As the infantry ascended it was seen how well the defence of the hill had been organised. The Gordon Highlanders and Kings Own Scottish Borderers ascending, as they did, on a direct attack, met with the greatest resistance and suffered most. *Sungar* after *sungar* was obstinately held; each *sungar* as it was rushed coming at once under the fire of the one above it. And here I may note the admirable service done by the Artillery and Maxim guns. Several attempts were made by the enemy to concentrate from above and hold the lower *sungars* and positions, but all such attempts were frustrated by the admirable practice of the Mountain Batteries and Maxim guns over the head of our advancing infantry.

Although at several points *sungars* were only carried by hand-to-hand fighting, the enemy were gradually driven from position to position, and eventually fled down the other slopes of the western hill, as the heads of the attacking columns reached the top, when the pass was captured and the fighting over, though they were pursued down the other side as soon as the men got together.

The action was begun at 8.30 a.m. and concluded at 2 p.m. The total numbers of the enemy are variously reported, but the actual numbers on the pass were probably about 10,000 to 12,000 men, some 3,000 armed, and the rest using rocks and stones. The enemy's loss was said by themselves to be about 500, and the road down the other side as covered with signs of numbers of wounded men having been carried away. Our loss was eleven men killed; and eight officers and thirty-nine men wounded. The 1st Brigade remained at the top of the pass, holding it, while the mules of the brigade passed up; but the path was so bad that only a few mules reached the top that night.

(Had the troops tried to make use of the path they would have suffered very severely, for the stonework of the *sungars* was found to be perforated with lateral slits, commanding every turn of the path. But the enemy had never calculated on a frontal attack straight up the face of the hill, and had neglected to provide themselves with vertical slits as well.)

In a subsequent despatch, Sir Robert Low adds:

In my despatch dated the 5th April I gave a brief account of the assault and capture of the Malakand Pass. It must be re-

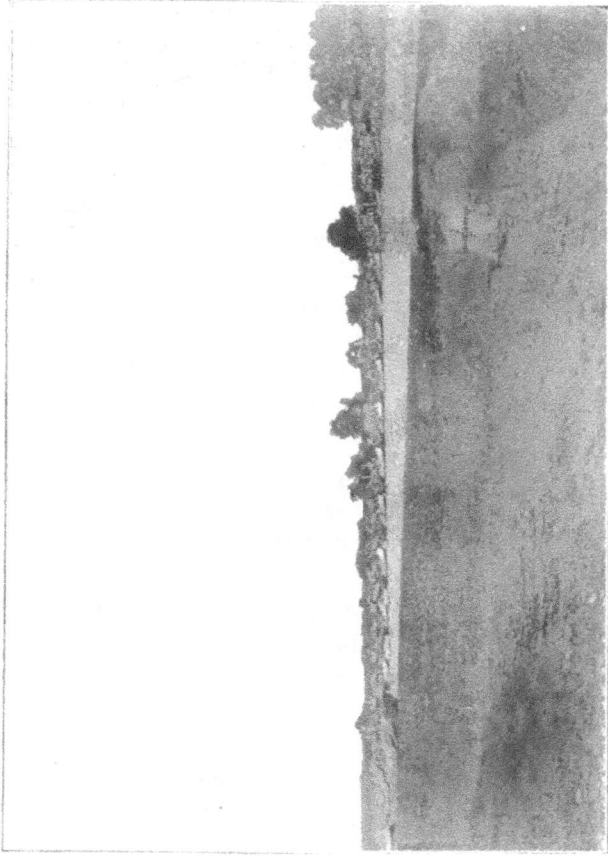

Bridge of Boats at Nowshera

membered that this was written only two days after the action, and, being based on my own observation, was necessarily incomplete. Thus I have to make an important correction in this report regarding one battalion—namely, the 4th Sikh Infantry, who did not remain stationary guarding the left flank of the advance, as I wrote, but joined throughout in the advance up to the highest peaks of the enemy's position, parallel with the Guides Infantry, having an equally arduous climb with them, and meeting with and carrying many *sungars* full of the enemy. During this advance officers and men alike distinguished themselves. In my original report also the enemy at the Malakand Pass were estimated at 12,000 men, of whom 3,000 were said to be armed with firearms, but we afterwards ascertained that the number armed with firearms was much larger.

The following day, 4th April, the 1st Brigade was ordered to descend the Malakand Pass into the Swat Valley, its place on the pass being taken by the 2nd Brigade, while the 3rd Brigade remained on the south side of the pass, pending the passage of the baggage and supplies of the rest of the force.

I may here allude to one of the most extraordinary coincidences within my experience. The height of the pass is about 1,000 feet from the valley below, and the track used by the hill people is most precipitous and goes straight up the hill by short zigzags, over boulders, and often under protruding crags; and when I saw it on the 3rd April it appeared to be impossible ever to make such a place fit for camels to carry loads over in any reasonable time. In the report of the Officer Commanding the King's Royal Rifle Corps on this day's action, he states that after going halfway up the hill he came upon 'an old pathway.'

On examination this turned out to be an old Buddhist road, disused for hundreds of years, but so well made originally that it took our Engineers and Sappers but two days to make it into a camel road from near Dargai, at the mouth of the pass, to the top. The discovery of this old and unknown road, on a good alignment and easily repaired, which came to our relief and enabled the force to advance in three days, when without it we should have been delayed many days, was certainly a remarkable stroke of good fortune.

THE SWAT VALLEY WITH MALAKAND PASS IN THE BACKGROUND

CHAPTER 14

Crossing of the Swat River
at Chakdara

By the time both the 1st and 2nd Brigades had reached the top of the pass it was 5 p.m. The 2nd Brigade had their rations with them, and their baggage was coming up behind as rapidly as possible. The 1st Brigade had no rations, and their baggage was behind that of the 2nd Brigade. An order was then given which led to great subsequent confusion and delay. The 2nd Brigade was recalled, and ordered to go back to camp at Dargai, and the 1st Brigade was ordered to go ahead. The path up the pass, at the best a very bad one, soon became hopelessly blocked with the hospital *doolies* and transport of the 2nd Brigade coming down the road, and the hospital and transport of the 1st Brigade going up it. The result was that the transport animals of the 2nd Brigade, after having got halfway up the pass, were put to the useless fatigue of going back all the way to Dargai, besides blocking the advance of the transport of the 1st Brigade, who had to bivouac on the top of the pass without food, and without even their greatcoats. Fortunately the night, though cold, was fine.

On the following morning, April 4th, the 1st Brigade was ordered to advance. The order did not reach General Kinloch till about ten o'clock, and before it came he had recalled the 37th Dogras from Khar at the bottom of the pass, where they had spent the night, as there was known to be a large gathering collected on a ridge known as the Amandarra, on one side of the road leading down from the pass into the Swat Valley. The Dogras got back to the rest of the brigade about twelve o'clock, and at one o'clock the whole brigade advanced, and the moment it got free of the pass it was fired upon by the enemy from the Amandarra ridge.

116

MALAKAND PASS

The Mountain Battery, under Major Dacres Cunningham, was then brought into action, and began shelling the *sungars*, and under cover of their fire the Bedfordshire Regiment moved forward to the hill where the enemy were collected, and drove them to the top of it, the rifles being lined out in front of the guns, which had been making wonderfully accurate shooting. It was impossible not to admire the courage displayed by the enemy, who exposed themselves most recklessly, the mullahs standing upon the *sungars* encouraging their followers, and waving large coloured banners. Those who were standing up on the *sungars* on the top of the hill showed clearly against the sky-line, and formed an excellent mark for the guns to aim at; in one case a shell being seen to strike a man with a banner fair in the middle of the body, and blow him and the banner high into the air.

The 37th Dogras were sent round to dislodge some others from a low spur to the left. This they did, and disappeared from view over the top of the spur. News was sent back that the enemy was advancing, and a squadron of the Guides cavalry, under Captain Adams, which had been sent over the pass to be attached to the 1st Brigade for the day, were sent to their relief. They went at a very fast pace, and as the ground was heavy the horses were ridden to a standstill by the time they arrived; but although the enemy were in great force they charged, and drove them back, killing about thirty. It had always been believed that the Swatis were much afraid of cavalry, and would never stand against them, and this charge, and the subsequent action on the Swat river, has amply confirmed this belief. The Dogras, who had been forty-eight hours without food, and who had endured great fatigue, behaved extremely well under very trying circumstances.

In the meantime the transport of the 1st Brigade was being gradually pushed on down the hill, and as soon as it was at the bottom the whole Brigade moved on to camp at Khar, which was not reached till after 7 p.m., the camp having to be pitched in the dark. The enemy were collected in such force on the surrounding hills that a night attack was expected, so the baggage was laagered, and the infantry lay with fixed bayonets all night, the guns being loaded with case, but no attempt at an attack was made.

The enemy are reported to have lost heavily on both days—their total loss being variously estimated from two to eight hundred. They probably did not lose more than three or four hundred at the outside, for though the guns made excellent shooting, the position was such a strong one naturally, with so much shelter behind the *sungars* and

MALAKAND PASS FROM FOOT OF KHAR VALLEY

rocks, that the shells lost much of the effect they would otherwise have had.

The consternation spread throughout the country by the capture of the pass was very great, for the Swatis have always looked upon all the three passes by which their country is entered, the Malakand, the Shahkot, and the Morah, as absolutely impregnable. Indeed it had been their proud boast that their *purdah* or curtain had never been lifted. It was impossible not to feel sorry for them, or not to admire their stubborn courage against such overwhelming odds; the more so as our quarrel was not with them but with Umra Khan. All we desired was a passage through their country. The few wounded whom they left behind had their wounds dressed, and if able to move were told to go back to their homes.

One lad was picked up very badly hurt. He was brought into Khar to be looked after. He said that he came from Barwa, Umra Khan's village in Jandol, and that he had been given a rifle and five rounds of ammunition, and told to go down to the Malakand Pass, and did not dare to refuse. His home was nearly a hundred miles away, and he had no relations or friends amongst the Swatis, which was why they had abandoned him when they retreated from the pass. A collection was made by some of the officers of the 1st Brigade, as much sympathy was felt for him; and he was sent off with thirty or forty *rupees*, and a blanket which one of the officers gave him, although he could ill spare it himself. Poor boy, he was badly hit, and it is very doubtful whether he ever managed to drag himself across the mountains to his home.

It was wonderful how cheerily the troops bore all the fatigue and privations they had to go through, for they were in want both of sleep and of food, but it did not damp their ardour in the least. The hospital arrangements were excellent. The wounded and sick were sent back at once as soon as they could be moved from the field hospitals at the front to the line of communication hospitals, and from there to the base hospitals at Nowshera and Peshawur. One of the wounded men brought on to the camp at Khar had his wounds dressed by his own people before they abandoned him. The dressing was a quaint example of primitive surgery. A *chappatie*, or thin flour cake, had been applied directly to the wound, and the skin of a freshly killed chicken bound round it. Needless to say the wound was not in a remarkably aseptic state.

They have however a very good idea of wooden splints. One man who had a gunshot wound in the arm had had it bound up with a fairly constructed cradle, similar to those generally used in veterinary practice. The wounds inflicted by the new Lee-Metford rifle were of great surgical interest, as they were almost the first that have come under observation since the adoption of the rifle. They seem to show the extremely small stopping power of the bullet, unless it happens to hit a bone or a vital part. One man had no less than three perforating wounds all in a perfectly clean condition, and although they had passed through the arm, thigh, and leg, the loss of blood had been very slight, and he was able to walk with the aid of a stick three miles to be attended. One of the Staff the day after the fight, found him in a village near Khar, and told him to go into the camp to be treated at the native field hospital; and this he did, going back to his village immediately afterwards.

Another man came into camp at Khar with two bullet wounds in his arm—one above the wrist, the other close to the shoulder. He had to wait in the camp for some time before he could be attended to, and one of the officers seeing him sitting there without much apparent pain, asked him if he could move his arm. He said he could quite easily, so he was given a stick, and flourished it over his head without any difficulty. The wounds were clean, and had not caused much inflammation. Another man had three wounds in the same leg, one above the other, probably from the Lee-Metford Maxim. He ran away for some distance after he had received the wounds, and was found and brought from four or five miles off into camp, had his wounds dressed, and then walked off again.

The net result of the observations made seems to be this: at a very short range of two or three hundred yards, the bullet has a sort of explosive action, and inflicts a large and jagged wound, not merely splintering a bone when it comes into contact with it, but absolutely pulverising it. At a medium range it makes a small clean wound, in one case boring a small hole clean through the bone without splintering it at all; and at a long range it again makes a bad wound, the wound at the place of exit being much larger and more jagged than at the place of entrance.

On the whole the Lee-Metford bullet does not seem to give very satisfactory results. It cannot be depended upon to stop a man in his charge, for the wound it inflicts is often insignificant. On the other hand, it sometimes produces a very terrible wound, almost like that of an explosive bullet.

It was pleasant to note how confident the people were that we

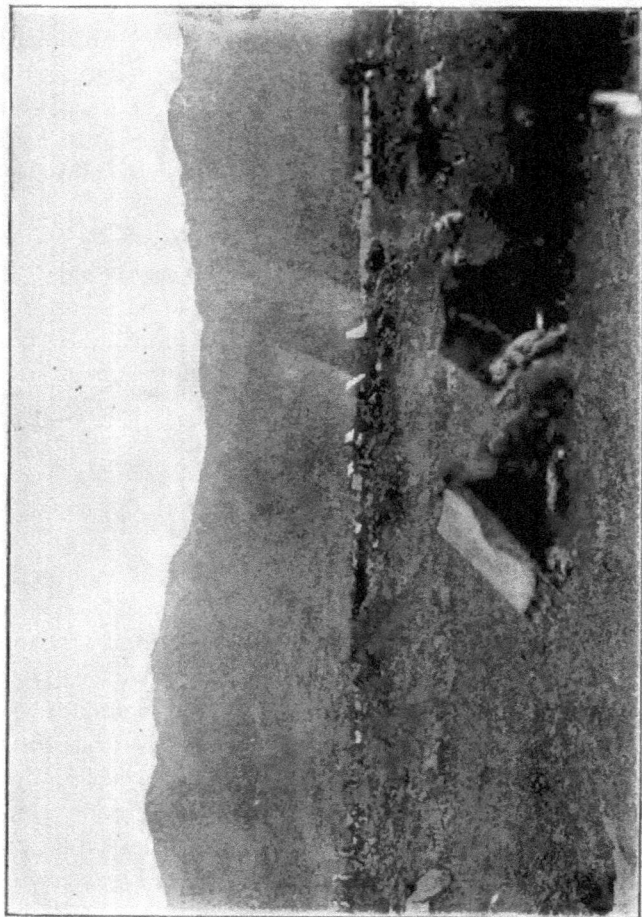

3RD BRIGADE CAMP AT KHAR

would not ill-treat them after they had once submitted; not only were cases of recent wounds brought in, but several people with chronic affections came in voluntarily for treatment.

Goître is very common, brought on probably by drinking snow-water, and so are eye affections.

On the 5th April the 1st Brigade remained all day in camp at Khar, the 2nd Brigade going eight miles further up the valley, and camping near Thana, the largest village in Swat. Heliographic communication was established between the two Brigades, and messages were constantly flashing from one to the other, to the great astonishment of the Swatis.

Mr. Rawlinson, the political officer with the 1st Brigade, overheard an amusing dialogue between two, who were waiting outside his tent for an interview. "Extraordinary devils, these Kafirs" (unbelievers), one of them said; "one army sits down and talks to the other army with the sun on a looking-glass (a very accurate description of the heliograph), and at night they put up two big lamps, and talk to each other with them."

"Well," said the other, "they can't do anything when it is cloudy, and there is no sun."

"Oh," replied the first speaker, "you may be sure they have some devilry they make use of then."

They had not yet divined the meaning of flag-signalling.

Early on the morning of the 7th Major Aylmer, escorted by a company of the King's Own Scottish Borderers, by the 4th Sikhs, and by the Maxim gun of the Devons under Captain Peebles, went down to the river to begin making a bridge. A heavy fire was opened on them from the heights on the other side; so General Waterfield ordered out the whole of the 2nd Brigade in support, and the 11th Bengal Lancers under Lieut.-colonel Scott, and the 15th Sikhs under Major Hadow were sent as a reinforcement from the 1st Brigade camp at Khar.

The enemy's position was a strong one. The Swat River at this part of the valley is divided into no less than five distinct streams, and the approach to it on both banks is soft and boggy. On the other side of the Shamlai Ferry, at the mouth of the Upper Swat Valley, is the village of Chakdara; and a little to the left of the village there is a rocky knoll three hundred feet in height, and about six hundred yards from the ford, which it effectually commands. The knoll and the village were both held in considerable force, and a continuous fusillade was maintained whilst the 11th Bengal Lancers were searching for a place to cross. The firing however was very wild, and there were hardly any casualties. No. 8 Mountain Battery, under Major Shirres, was brought into action, and shelled both village and knoll continuously for some time. A week or two after the engagement some of the villagers picked up an unexploded shell. They wanted to see what was inside it, and were trying to break it open with a stone, when it exploded and killed four of them, and wounded five others badly.

About eleven o'clock two squadrons of the 11th Bengal Lancers and one squadron of the Guides Cavalry succeeded in finding a ford. As soon as they gained the opposite bank the enemy stopped firing, and fled precipitately up the valley. The Cavalry pursued them for five or six miles, as far as Uch at the mouth of the Katgola Pass, and killed about a hundred. Amongst the fugitives were thirty or forty horsemen, forming the escort of Mahommed Shah Khan, the brother of Umra Khan, by whom the enemy was commanded.

Another squadron of the 11th Bengal Lancers, and one of the Guides, forded the river exactly opposite the village, which they oc-cupied. They were followed immediately afterwards by the infantry. The enemy had abandoned both the village and the isolated knoll to the left of it. The latter was said to have been held by two hundred of Umra Khan's *sepoys* armed with Martini-Henrys. Their position was naturally so strong that if they had held it with any determination they must have inflicted severe loss, for the stream was very rapid, and the water being over the men's waists they were obliged to go across with locked arms in groups of four or five to avoid being washed away; and in spite of this two of the 4th Sikhs were drowned. The ground, too, on the other side was so soft that they sank in up to their knees. But though the enemy are said to have had nearly five thousand men present, there was no heart in the stand they made, and our loss proved to be quite trivial.

The village was found to be entirely deserted by the inhabitants, who fled to the hills as soon as the troops began to cross the river. It was occupied that night by the 4th Sikhs and 15th Sikhs, and on the following day the whole of the 2nd Brigade moved over from Thana, and camped in and around it. The river was then quite fordable even for baggage animals, and more than three thousand mules and a number of camels were got safely over without one being lost; but a day or two afterwards the water rose so much from the rapid melting of the snow on the mountains that several camels were drowned, and a permanent bridge had to be begun at once.

MULBERRY GROVE—CHAKDARA

SWAT RIVER AND TEMPORARY TRESTLE BRIDGE

Directly the Swat Valley was fairly in our hands the people began to show a friendly feeling, and to come in with sheep, fowls, eggs, and milk for sale. Fowls were at first eight for a *rupee*, and eggs six for an *anna*, but the price of everything soon went up with the demand.

The Swat Valley is throughout exceedingly fertile. It is covered with luxuriant crops of green barley, clover, and Lucerne grass, and cultivation by irrigation has been brought to great perfection.

Professor Darmesteter made a very interesting translation of a Pathan ballad describing the Swat Valley, which, until this expedition, was to Europeans a closed country. It is rather long, but I will quote one of the verses, as it gives a really very accurate description of the valley.

> *Çvat s'engage à produire toute sorte de riz. Il produit également le maïs et le blé, les haricots et les fèves. Il ne connaît pas l'orge, ses paniers sont vides d'orge. La terre de Çvat est une terre d'or, mais ses habitants sont des mendiants. Ils sont toujours à partager la terre, et toujours à se faire la guerre entre eux—aussi n'est elle point bien cultivée, étant toujours à changer la main. Le pays de Çvat est froid. J'y étais toujours à l'aise. Les eaux sont purs et fraîches et coulent claires. Au bord des rivières s'alignent des forêts de platanes. Les montagnes sont couvertes de pins immenses. Les monts Morai et Ilam sont froids, allez les visiter. En été il faut y allumer le feu dans les maisons. L'hiver de Peshawur c'est de l'été du Mont Ilam.*

He gives the following statement with regard to the very curious custom which exists in Swat of the whole of the lands of a village being exchanged every few years for those of another village.

> *Par la coutume du Vesh, la terre de la tribu est divisée en lots entre les clans, et la distribution des lots est changée à des époques périodiques, de sorte que la terre est en mouvement perpetuel.*

CHAPTER 15

The Guides Fight

General Low's despatch continues the story of the advance:—

On the 9th April headquarters crossed the Swat River and joined the 2nd Brigade at Chakdara, the 3rd Brigade encamping on the opposite bank at Aladand.

On the 10th headquarters and the 2nd Brigade marched to Gumbat, crossing the Katgola Pass. The 3rd Brigade crossed the Swat River to Chakdara, the 1st Brigade under Brigadier-General Kinloch, C.B., being left to guard the Swat Valley and the communications. On the 11th headquarters and the 2nd Brigade reached the Panjkora River at Sado Ferry. There are two routes to the ferry from Gumbat, one by the Shago Kas defile, the other by the Kamrani Pass. The former route was taken, as the pass route was reported unfit for camels, but the Shago Kas road in its original state was such an intricate one, and was so very bad, that all the labour of the force was afterwards put on to the other to make it fit for animals. Owing to the extreme difficulty of the defile the baggage did not get into camp till very late that night, being fired into several times *en route*.

Before I moved on from the Swat River an advanced guard had been sent on ahead, consisting of the 11th Bengal Lancers, two squadrons of the Guides Cavalry, the Guides Infantry and the 4th Sikhs, which had arrived at Sado on the 10th. The cavalry forded the river and reconnoitred up the Bajour Valley on the 10th, finding Umra Khan's forts held, and on that evening owing to the river rising, they experienced considerable difficulty in recrossing to the left bank. On my arrival it was clear that nothing but a bridge could get the troops across, and this was

127

SWAT RIVER AND CHAKDARA VILLAGE.

CAMP SADO AND PANJKORA RIVER, WITH JANDOL VALLEY AND SCENE
OF GUIDES' FIGHT IN THE DISTANCE.

at once commenced by Major Aylmer, V.C., Royal Engineers, with the 4th Company, Bengal Sappers and Miners, under the direction of Colonel Leach, D.S.O., Commanding Royal Engineers with the force.

The bridge was built on raft-piers constructed from the logs lying on the banks of the river. On the evening of the 12th men on foot could cross, and there being every hope of my being able to cross the troops and their baggage the following day, the Guides Infantry were passed over to cover the bridge, and formed an entrenched post at the apex of a re-entering angle of the right bank, on which the end of the bridge rested. This post had a level space of some hundreds of yards in front and being with its surroundings thoroughly commanded at short range by the high ground on the left bank, was extremely strong.

On the morning of the 13th, between 3 and 5 a.m., an unexpected misfortune happened. The river rose suddenly and brought down large logs of timber which broke the bridge, and as the current increased at the same time to such an extent as to make a raft-bridge useless, it was seen at once that the only resource was to make a suspension bridge.

A suitable place, about two miles down the stream from the site of the raft-bridge, was accordingly selected, and a design was adopted by which the cables of the bridge were to be made of many strands of telegraph wire. Work was commenced immediately, but the bridge could not be expected to be ready for three or four days. The site selected being, as I have said, about two miles downstream, a new road was required along the hillside on the right bank to the mouth of the Bajour Valley, which road could only be commenced when men could be passed over the river.

On the morning of the 13th Lieutenant Edwardes was sent into the camp by Umra Khan. He said that he had been well treated, and that Umra Khan had promised to send Fowler in a day or two afterwards. The Guides had been ordered overnight to burn some of the villages on the opposite bank of the river from which firing had been persistently kept up upon the transport, and proceeded accordingly to do so. When the bridge however was washed away the watchmen on the hill tops sent news of what had happened up the Jandol Valley to Mandia, and the mullahs there roused the fanatical ardour of the people by proclaiming that *Allah* had delivered a regiment into their hands with all its rifles and ammunition.

I have been kindly allowed to take the following extract from the diary of Surgeon-Lieutenant D. W. Sutherland, the medical officer to the Guides, who was with them all through the fight that ensued.

13th April, 1895.

This morning, at daybreak, the Guides set out to burn the villages of the Utman Kneyls, and of the people of the lower part of the Jandol Valley, as punishment for shots fired during the night, and on the rearguard of the 2nd Brigade on the afternoon and night of the 11th instant.

The regiment moved on in separate companies, first over the near hill, dismantling and burning each village met with, and then afterwards on the left side of the Jandol Valley for several miles, until no further villages could be seen. Hiding in the valley were about 100 cows, buffaloes, and donkeys, and these were seized and driven back to the camp on the Panjkora River.

Some of the Guides companies were fired upon from villages on the right bank of the Jandol stream, so after burning all the villages on the left side, the Guides crossed the river to crown the hills, and complete their work on the right side.

While fording the Jandol stream, which was about knee deep, a few shots were fired from the hills above, but the companies protecting the crossing killed the few firers with a volley or two. The high hills on the right overlooking the Jandol Valley were then crowned, and a dozen or more Utman Kheyl villages lying behind were burnt. The hills were then held for some hours. A beautiful view was obtained through the Chigarkas Pass of the Talash Valley behind, and at the further end of the valley the hills of Swat could be distinctly seen through the Katgola Pass. Behind us to the left lay the Panjkora Valley, where the 2nd Brigade was encamped, and in front opened up the Jandol Valley, which led up for several miles, and then turned sharp to the right towards Barwa, Umra Khan's chief town.

At the end of the valley, Miankalai and several forts could be distinctly seen. Up the valley a large force could be seen gathered on the low spurs and plain near Mandai, with red and white standards. These then split up into two columns and advanced towards us, one on either side of the Jandol stream, and our retreat was hopelessly cut off by the bridge having been swept away in the early morning, and the river being too deep and the current too strong to ford. The G.O.C. was signalled to for instructions, and in reply came the order to fall back upon the river directly in the rear, while the brigade would cover the retreat from the opposite bank.

At this time the main body of the Guides was on a high bank on the right, while companies were out under Lieutenant H. W. Codrington and Lieutenant P. E. Lockhart, burning the villages below in the valley and towards the river. The order to retreat was signalled to them, and the men collected, but before this could be done the enemy were within range, and had opened fire upon us with rifles and *jezails*.

The right column of the enemy were soon upon us, and our position became very critical. When all the men were ready, we slowly retreated down two parallel slopes, the enemy taking the hill over us as we retreated, and following us down. They numbered several thousands to our single regiment. When half-way down we could see the left column of the enemy running across the plain to gain the hill and try and cut us off from our camp. On the opposite side of the river the 2nd Brigade got into position, and soon the Maxim guns of the Gordons and K.O.S.B.'s, and the Mountain Battery, were considerably help-ing us. Still the enemy advanced, firing rapidly, and coming near enough to hurl stones, some of which struck our men.

Our right party, under Lieutenant Lockhart, who had been keeping up a flank fire on the enemy from their slope, and materially covering our retreat, first reached the foot of the hill and hastened to oppose the enemy coming up on the flank. Lieutenant Codrington's party early reaching the river, and seeing the engagement above, hurried up to our help. Slowly down the slope we went, yielding position after position only when compelled to do so, and at last reached the lowest posi-tion on the slope, beyond which there was a steep descent. This position was held for some time under a hot fire by Colonel Battye, while those who had reached the bottom were formed up in the field below.

Then the position was yielded, the descent being covered by fire from our men who had been formed up in the field by Lieutenant Cockerill, of the Intelligence Department, who had been attached to us for the day, assisted by Lieutenants Co-drington, Lockhart, Maxwell, Stewart, and Bogle. Colonel Battye was the last to retreat, and while retreating slowly was shot through the body, and fell mortally wounded. Seeing him fall, the Guides Afridi Company fixed their bayonets and charged the enemy up the slope, killing and wounding many. Then they retired, and the enemy gained the position once more. They were then kept in check by a steady Maxim fire from the brigade, aided by the Gordons, K.O.S.B.'s, and 4th Sikhs' fire, and the shells of the Mountain Battery from the further side of the Panjkora River.

Carrying the colonel's body, and that of another man who had been shot in the head, we slowly retreated back to our old camp in the bed of the river, but before we reached it the left column of the enemy had gained the hills above us to our left. Lieutenant Lloyd Johnson, with two companies who had been left in camp, advanced against them, and our men, replenishing their ammunition and leaving the wounded in the rear, also went forward against them, being assisted by the Maxim gun of the Devons, which had crossed one of the small branches of the river and got into position on an island, and materially aided us on the left, the right column being held in check by the 2nd Brigade. The Guides remained at the foot of the hills, keeping the enemy at bay while entrenchments were being dug, and stone breastworks piled up in camp. Then they slowly retired, their retirement being covered by a party of the 23rd Pioneers and K.O.S.B.'s, Gordons, and 4th Sikhs, firing from the heights on the further bank.

Once back in camp all lay down in the entrenchments, and returned the fire of the enemy from the hills above us, about 600 or 800 yards to our front. The enemy soon got the range of the camp, and shots were poured in upon us. Soon the two Maxim guns of the Devons, under Captain Peebles and Lieutenant Kane, were floated across on rafts to our aid, and established on either side of our entrenchments fronting the enemy. Then night fell and the firing continued, and throughout the night we all lay behind our entrenchments, receiving and returning shots every moment. The enemy were lit up now and then by star shells from the Mountain Battery, and a rush on the camp consequently prevented.

The first shell set fire to some brushwood, which burnt for some time. Still, some of the enemy came very near, and were shot about forty yards only from our camp. On the hills in front some sharpshooters made excellent shooting at us, and every bullet almost reached the camp, the number falling in the vicinity of the mess-table being especially noticeable.

After a weary night of anxiety and watching the dawn at length approached, and just before we heard the music of pipes above us on the hills, and after that received only an occasional shot, the main body having marched away, having been recalled, it is thought, by Umra Khan, who had sent a messenger in with a letter in the morning, asking:

(1) What have I done to offend the *Sircar?*

(2) How long will the offence last? and

(3) What is my punishment likely to be?

A reply was sent back, and it is thought that upon the receipt of that he recalled his men. Still, after dawn came, a few *badmashes* remained on the hill, and kept firing on the camp with Sniders and Martini-Henrys. About five o'clock they seemed to increase in number, and wounded one of the Devons in the leg. Immediately afterwards Captain Peebles, of the Devons' Maxim gun, fell near the mess-table, shot through the abdomen. Then orders came for the Guides to clear the hills, which they at once did, driving the enemy before them and securing the summits. Not until the afternoon of that day did the men obtain any food, having fasted more than forty-eight hours. Some of the *sepoys* had fasted even longer.

The Guides remained on the hills that day, and were joined in the afternoon by the 4th Sikhs, who had come over on the rafts, and the two regiments bivouacked together on the hills behind the breastworks. During the night a thunderstorm came on, with very heavy rain, which lasted some hours and soaked us thoroughly.

The enemy were so close to the Guides when they dropped from the spur of the hill into the field below, that they were actually hurling rocks down upon them, and it was only their own steadiness that saved them from a terrible disaster. Had they shown any signs of confusion the enemy would have been right in amongst them, and the guns on the opposite bank would then have been unable to cover them; but they retired as slowly and deliberately as though they had been on parade. Colonel Battye's death was a serious loss. He had a wide experience of frontier warfare, and was greatly beloved by the Guides, who would have followed him anywhere. His body was taken down by an escort of cavalry, and was buried in Mardan, where he had spent so many years of his life. Captain Peebles also was an officer who could ill be spared. He was a keen and rising soldier, and a recognised authority upon the Maxim gun, for which he had invented a carriage.

THE FORT AT SADO.

CHAPTER 16

Skirmish at Ghoban

An interesting piece of information was elicited some time after the fight. The older men wished to make a night attack, the favourite method of Pathan warfare, but were overruled by the younger men, who wished to try and cut the Guides off before they could get down from the ridge on which they then were. This attack having failed, the greybeards said it was their turn to try what they could do. So about two thousand of them crept cautiously down into a small ravine, about fifty yards from the Guides' camp, and were gathering themselves together for a rush, when a star shell from the Mountain Battery was exploded right over them, showing the Guides clearly where they were, and astonishing them so much that they lay quite still for some considerable time. They were again preparing to attack, when another shell exploded over them, and, to use their own words, *"in a moment all became day,"* and they abandoned the attempt altogether.

If they had attacked they would probably have inflicted serious loss, for a night attack by so large a body of men is difficult to repel; but they would have had a very warm reception from the Maxims under Captain Peebles and Lieutenant Kane. As it was they must have suffered severely from the heavy fire poured in on them by the 2nd Brigade during their attack upon the Guides. It disheartened them altogether, and they never made any serious stand again. They said themselves, "We are quite ready to meet you in the open with *tulwars*, but we can do nothing against your devil-guns, which kill us from a mile and a-half off."

The episode of the star shell reminds me of a story I was told in Alexandria. A night or two before the bombardment, Sir Beauchamp Seymour suddenly turned the electric light upon the forts, to the great consternation of the Arabs, who fled in all directions, thinking the moon was falling down upon them. Would not a portable electric light apparatus be of great service in these frontier expeditions, where night attacks are always to be expected? It was employed, I believe, in the South African expeditions, and found exceedingly useful.

It was evident that there were a good many deserters and discharged *sepoys* from the Indian army in the ranks of the enemy, for the words "present"—"fire" were distinctly audible, followed by a volley.

After the Guides had retired to their camp on the beach, the Pathans turned their attention to the brigade on the other side of the river, which had been within easy range all through the fight. Just before sunset they poured in a number of volleys, and hit several men. Captain O'Leary, of the Royal Irish Fusiliers, who was in charge of the signallers, had a narrow escape. He was struck sideways in the chest by a bullet which glanced off his accoutrements, bruising him a good deal, but not doing him any damage.

One of the ambulance-bearers received a curious wound. He was squatting down in the position in which a native always sits, and a bullet drilled a hole through both legs and both arms. Surgeon-Colonel O'Connor told me that after his wounds had been dressed he sat up and wanted to sing a song. He had had a little brandy, which had very likely got into his head; but it is astonishing how pluckily natives bear the pain of a wound. At Ghoban I saw one of the *sowars* of the 11th Bengal Lancers, who had been shot through the thigh about an hour before, try to get up to salute one of his officers, who told him not to move. "Oh," he said, "it is all right, *sahib*; it is only a flesh wound. It has not touched the bone." He had ridden back with the regiment after being hit, without saying a word about it, though the force of the concussion when the bullet struck him must have been considerable.

It was necessary to make another bridge in place of the one which had been washed away; and Major Aylmer in forty-eight hours succeeded in throwing a suspension bridge over the river about two miles lower down, at a place where the stream was narrower. It had to be made roughly out of telegraph wire, but it proved strong enough not only to enable the 2nd and 3rd Brigades to cross with all their transport, but to bear for weeks the whole of the traffic from the line of communications, until there had been time to supplement it by another and stronger bridge; indeed, it continued in constant use throughout the remainder of the campaign.

While the suspension bridge was being made, communication was maintained with the other bank, at the site of the old bridge, by means of a skin raft, propelled by two native boatmen. This raft was taking across two of the Devonshires and one of the 4th Sikhs, when it upset. The other men were drowned, but one of the Devonshires and a boatman managed to hold on to it, and were carried rapidly downstream towards the suspension bridge. General Gatacre saw the raft overturn, and immediately galloped down to the new bridge as fast as he could, reaching it before the overturned raft got there, and had a rope stretched across the river, which the men on the raft caught hold of. The boatman managed to swim ashore, but the Devonshire man was pulled under water by the strength of the current, and would have been drowned, had not Major Aylmer been let down in a cradle, and managed to pull him ashore. The remainder of the campaign was uneventful.

General Low's despatch gives the following clear and succinct account of it:—

During the 14th the remainder of the 4th Sikhs crossed on *mussuck*-rafts, and joined the Guides Infantry, and a strong position on spurs on the other side of the river and to the north of the Ushiri stream was occupied by these two battalions. The crossing on the few small rafts at my disposal became every moment more difficult and slower, owing to the river continuing to rise. On the night of the 14th very bad weather set in, and rain continued all that night, and through the day and night of the 15th, much delaying work on the suspension bridge, and the rising water approached nearer and nearer to its piers.

On the morning of the 16th, with the Swat River in my rear, reported also to be steadily rising, and the bridge over it, on which I depended for supplies, hardly completed and of doubtful stability, with the Panjkora River in front of me rising into a tremendous torrent and threatening the new suspension bridge, the two remaining rafts (one had been overturned and two damaged by bullets) unable longer to pass over supplies, the situation was one of grave anxiety.

The Guides Infantry and the 4th Sikhs with them had the previous evening been ordered, as the only means of feeding them, to be ready to park their ammunition and baggage in the entrenched post of the Guides Infantry, and make their way to the suspension bridge, so that they might recross before the bridge was swept away; and things looked so serious on the morning of the 16th that they were ordered to commence this movement.

When, however, I visited the bridge early on the morning of the 16th, I was informed that no further rise had taken place in the last three or four hours; and, during the time that I was there, the water, if anything, fell, and the rain ceased. I therefore sent orders to the Guides Infantry and 4th Sikhs to stand fast. At noon it was clear that the water was falling, and that the danger was over for the time. But the necessity for a bridge above high flood-level was evidently urgent, and the Commandant, Royal Engineers, put it in hand at once; and I trust it may be ready before the river rises again.

Lieutenant Fowler, Royal Engineers, was on this day sent in by Umra Khan.

On the morning of the 17th the two brigades were ordered to advance. One squadron of the Guides Cavalry marched at an early hour to reconnoitre up the valley towards Miankila, under the orders of Brigadier-General Blood, C.B., and the 11th Bengal Lancers and the two infantry brigades followed across the river.

At 10 a.m., after the troops of the 3rd Brigade (which was leading) had crossed, I received a message from Brigadier-General Blood that the enemy were in sight near the village of Miankila, and were advancing from thence. The road on the right bank of the Panjkora River from the bridge up to the open valley was only a footpath fit for mules, over which every man and animal had to go in single file, horses having to be led, and it was clear that both brigades could not hope to get across and move up to the scene of action during the day.

I therefore directed Brigadier-General Waterfield to pass over the baggage of the 3rd Brigade which could reach that brigade before night, and then only to cross the bridge with his own brigade and its transport, and to join me the first thing next morning.

Then pushing on myself, I reached Ghoban just as the 3rd Brigade were going into action. The enemy occupied the hills on the left or southern side of the valley, and held the villages of Gulderi and Andak to the west on some bluffs above the river and the hills to the south of the Ushiri. The 4th Gurkhas were directed up the southern hills and then to move along them to the west: the Seaforth Highlanders being on the slopes below them, and the 25th Punjab Infantry in support. Two companies of the Buffs occupied the hills to the north, with No. 2 (Dera-jat) Mountain Battery in action on a knoll in the centre, and the remainder of the Buffs in reserve.

While the infantry cleared the southern hills, the 11th Bengal Lancers advanced up the centre of the valley to a small village, Gosam, where their horses got protection from the enemy's fire, but the cavalry got no opportunity of charging, the ground in their front being too broken. The enemy on this occasion did not show the bold front of previous days, but retired as the infantry advanced, and though the guns were sent forward about 1,000 yards to hasten their retreat, the loss of the enemy was not great. Throughout the action the troops were well handled by Brigadier-General Gatacre, D.S.O.

On the morning of the 18th Brigadier-General Waterfield with the 2nd Brigade joined me, and the 2nd and 3rd Brigades advanced against Miankilaand Mundar. The latter, a fort on the left bank of the Jandol River, is the home of Umra Khan, and it was expected that he would make a final stand at one of these places. Both were, however, deserted, and it was reported that Umra Khan had fled towards Asmar, and had asked for an asylum from the *Amir* of Kabul, I may add that he has been a fugitive ever since.

The same afternoon Brigadier-General Gatacre with the Buffs, the 4th Gurkhas, half of No. 4 Company, Bengal Sappers and Miners, No. 2 (Derajat) Mountain Battery, and the two Maxim guns of the Devonshire Regiment pushed on to Barwa, *en route* for Dir and Chitral with twenty days' supplies; and the remainder of the brigade, *viz.*, the Seaforth Highlanders and the 25th Punjab Infantry, were taken on by me on the morning of the 20th to Kambat (called Chashma at first) at the foot of the Janbatai Pass.

On the afternoon of April 20th, Brigadier-General Gatacre sent a message back to me that Major Deane, chief political officer (who accompanied him), had received news that the garrison of Chitral was reduced to great straits, and that the mines of the enemy had reached to within ten yards of the walls of the fort, and he suggested that he should advance rapidly with a small body of 500 men. To this I consented, as being the only way

VIEW OF SNOWS FROM JANBATAI PASS

SHER AFZUL'S ARMY OUTSIDE DIR FORT, GUARDED BY SENTRIES OF
THE GORDON HIGHLANDERS

of passing quickly through the intricate country we were now traversing, and the only chance of rescuing the garrison.

To support him while out of communication, I sent forward on the 21st the Seaforth Highlanders with all the supplies I could collect, and arranged to move on myself with the 25th Punjab Infantry when more supplies arrived. On the following day, the 21st, reassuring news came regarding the garrison of Chitral Fort, *viz*., that it was holding out on the 17th, and later that Sher Afzul had abandoned the siege and had absconded; this was confirmed on the following day, the 22nd.

At that time it was not known whether the relief of Chitral Fort had been effected by Colonel Kelly, or by the occupation of Kila Drosh by the *Khan* of Dir acting under my orders, or by the advance of my force and the defeat of Umra Khan. Probable it was the result of all three, but it is now known that Colonel Kelly was the first to arrive at Chitral, on April 20th.

When this news was received, Brigadier-General Gatacre was directed not to advance hurriedly, but with due consideration for his troops. The Janbatai Pass (7,400 feet) was found to be a very difficult one, and the hills beyond it were very much more difficult to traverse than any that had yet been passed over, and it was only possible to move over this pass by single battalions at a time.

On my arrival at Dir on April 25th, Brigadier-General Gatacre was crossing the Lowarai Pass, which was accomplished by the Buffs and half a battalion of the 4th Gurkhas on the 26th and 27th without any loss, though it was only done by all the troops following the example of Brigadier-General Gatacre himself and exhibiting the most determined perseverance and energy. The troops above named, *viz*., the Buffs and half a battalion of the 4th Gurkhas, are now at Ashreth in Chitral, where they have been ordered to halt pending further orders, as with the capture of Sher Afzul, who was brought into my camp a prisoner on the 27th, peace in the Chitral Valley is re-established.

I would before concluding allude to the message sent to the troops of this force by His Excellency the Commander-in-Chief in India, published in Divisional Orders of April 21st, also those from Her Most Gracious Majesty, the Queen Empress of India, and His Excellency the Viceroy, published in Divisional Orders of April 29th, which congratulated them on the success

Officers' Bivouac on the Janbatai Pass.

which had so far attended their efforts, and praised them for their endurance. These messages were much appreciated by the troops, and assuredly they were never better earned, as His Excellency the Commander-in-Chief is aware. The troops of this force had unavoidably to start in lighter order than I believe any large body of troops have ever done before in India. They have been exposed to great hardships owing to the month being an unusually stormy one,

When not fighting or marching, every man has laboured with the greatest cheerfulness all day on road-making, and altogether the month has been one of continued exertion, and cheerful self-denial and devotion, under circumstances of unusual difficulty and hardship.

I cannot speak too highly in this respect of the conduct of all ranks, both British and Native.

CHAPTER 17

March of the 3rd Brigade Over the Janbatai and Lowarai Passes

General Gatacre's brigade had an unmolested march from Barwar to Chitral, but a march full nevertheless of varied experiences, and one that tried the endurance of the troops to the utmost.

From Jandol, the road—steep in places, but on the whole an excellent mountain road—crosses the Janbatai Pass, which is 7,400 feet in height, and from the summit of which a magnificent view is obtained. "*Janbatai*" means "The Life of Stone," and it is easy to understand how it has been acquired. Behind, the fertile valleys of Jandol, Talash, and Nawagai, convey a sense of fullness and plenty and ease; in front, a tangled network of confined valleys with almost precipitous sides, terminating in the lofty range that forms the frontier of Chitral, impress the imagination with an aspect of rugged grandeur.

When Umra Khan came back from Kila Drosh bringing Edwards and Fowler with him, he seated himself on the roof of a house near the summit of the pass, with the two officers beside him. He asked them what they thought of his country, and then remained absorbed for some time in silent contemplation of the fair land he could not but feel would not be his much longer.

Lower Swat and Jandol are nearly treeless valleys, the hillsides being either bare, or, where there are springs, irrigated almost up to the very summit; but directly the Janbatai Pass is crossed, the nature of the scenery changes entirely. The valleys, though cramped and narrow, are exceedingly fertile; the villages are surrounded with fruit-trees, and the hills are clothed with dense forests.

About ten miles from Dir the Janbatai River flows into the Panjkora, the scenery at the point of junction being exceedingly fine. Dir itself is a large, tumbledown fort, in which the *khan* lives. It is perched up on the side of a hill at a height of 5,650 feet, and close by, on a neighbouring hill, is a straggling, dirty village called Arriankot, which contains about 500 houses, and is chiefly inhabited by Hindu traders. For the last four or five years it has been under the sway of Mahomed Shah, the younger brother of Umra Khan, the same man who opposed us so unsuccessfully at the passage of the Swat River at Chakdara. Upon his defeat Mahomed Sharif, the hereditary *khan*, who had been living in exile in Swat, advanced rapidly over the Laram Pass to Dir, At first the people were a little doubtful whether to join him or not, but when news was received of the utter collapse of the Jandolis at Sado, they came over to him at once. Mahomed Shah had not even time to save his family and personal effects. His wives fell into the hands of Mahomed Sharif, who detained them in Dir. This seemed to Mahomed Shah so intolerable a piece of oppression that he wrote to Mahomed Sharif threatening, if they were not given up to him at once, to proceed instantly to Calcutta, and there lay the matter before the Company Bahadur. Rather a quaint appeal from a man actually in arms against us!

As far as Dir the road was fairly good, but on reaching Dir it was found that the road beyond, up to the Lowarai Pass, would be quite impracticable for mules until the sappers and miners, under Major Aylmer and Lieutenant Lubbock, had straightened it out a bit, so they were sent on ahead with two hundred of the Buffs and one hundred of the Gurkhas, taking with them three days' rations, carried by *coolies*.

It was not only that the road was bad, requiring a good deal of blasting to make it passable for pack animals, but the river had to be bridged in four places before Mirga could be reached. In three days, however, both bridges and road were ready,, and the mules were able to get along without any difficulty to Mirga, a squalid village situated about half way between Dir and the foot of the pass, at a height of 8,400 feet.

The sappers and miners had indeed by far the hardest work of any one in the force—their work was never ending. They were always half a march ahead, making the road passable; so they had both shorter commons and greater exposure.

From Mirga we marched another five miles to Gujar, where we came upon the snow. It was very cold, with a keen biting wind, and to add to our discomfort, there was a thunderstorm during the night,

FORT CHUTIATAN AND PANJKORA RIVER; LOOKING SOUTH.

with heavy showers of sleet. It was found that there was still a good deal of snow upon the pass—about four miles of it—so the sappers and miners, and some of the Buffs and Gurkhas, were sent on by torchlight in the middle of the night, before the snow got soft, to beat down a track for the mules. They had a wretchedly uncomfortable march in the drizzling rain, but did what had to be done, and the mules were able to get up to the summit of the pass without much difficulty. Then the real struggle began. There was a steep glissade of more than a thousand feet, down which both men and mules slipped as best they could. One of the officers had a curious escape from being badly hurt. He was tobogganing quietly down, when he happened to glance back over his shoulder and saw a mule immediately behind him, coming down with such velocity that he had only just time to throw himself on one side before it shot over the place where he had been the moment before.

It is recorded that when Timur invaded India in 1398, he came across these mountains, and had to be lowered down the steep snow slopes attached to a rope. We had no one with us of sufficient value for that, but the fat commissariat clerk, a Bengali Babu, who weighed nineteen stone, was put into a tarpaulin and shot safely to the bottom. The hospital "*doolies*" were a great trouble. They are so heavy that they require a great many men to carry them, and being stiff and unwieldy they could not be manoeuvred with the rapidity which was required.

A few weeks ago, (as at time of first publication), Major F. C. Carter, in a paper on mountain warfare made the following remarks:—

Another medical question of some importance in mountain warfare is the carrying of wounded men. The stretchers now in use are by no means suitable for steep hillsides, as there is nothing to prevent the sick man from sliding off the canvas, either in front, in rear, or on either side. On two occasions, even when carried with the greatest care, I have seen this happen to a wounded man, thus endangering life and causing fearful and unnecessary pain. It strikes me that some sort of arrangement consisting of merely a net or canvas hammock, carried with or without pole, would be preferable. I do not think such an arrangement has ever been tested on service. After all, it is but modernising the old idea of the infantry sash.

This is exactly what was done by Surgeon–Major Shewen, of the

FORT CHUTIATAN AND PANJKORA RIVER; LOOKING NORTH.

THE LOWARAI PASS.

Indian Medical Staff. He found that it would be impossible to get his *doolies* over the pass as they were. So he had the heavy framework taken out, the *doolie* being practically converted into a hammock slung to a pole, so light that a sick man inside it could be carried with ease by two men, and a great deal more comfortable to lie in than in its original condition.

After the snow was over we still had a long and toilsome descent of five or six miles to Ashreth, the whole march from Gujar to Ashreth being about fourteen miles. But in spite of the fatigue and exposure the health of the men was wonderfully good; when we reached Ashreth the only men on the sick-list being two of the Buffs and three of the Gurkhas. Some of the followers, however, suffered a good deal. I had two Pathan servants, Aleem Khan, a discharged *sepoy*, and Mahomed Shah, a *mullah* or priest. They both had bad attacks of fever, and Aleem Khan became so ill that I was unable to take him over the pass, and had to send him back from Gujar. Mahomed Shah insisted on going on, and managed to get down to Ashreth; but there he became so ill, in spite of heavy doses of quinine, that I was obliged to send him back with one of the return convoys. Before he went he begged me to let him have a pen and ink and some strips of paper. I thought he wanted to write to his home, and asked if he would like me to get him a postcard. "No," he replied, "I don't want to send a letter. I want to write some verses from the *Koran* on the strips of paper. I shall stick them on different parts of my body, and it may be that I shall become well." He did so, but I regret to say, became worse.

I asked General Gatacre to what cause he attributed the unusual immunity of the troops from sickness. His answer was, "Plenty of work and very little rum." Not that General Gatacre is a teetotaller. He is not, but he believes that men can inure themselves to hardship, and that if they are constantly given rum they get to crave for it, and in time can't do without it, and it then loses the stimulating effect it should have when really required. We certainly had very little. It was only served out in the 3rd Brigade once or twice during the whole march; after exceptionally trying periods of exposure. And there was certainly no lack of work. The men were always road-making if they were not actually marching. They naturally grumbled a little, but the splendid condition they were in when they reached Chitral was a sufficient justification of General Gatacre's belief that if men are allowed to be idle during the intervals of marching, they become ill.

General Gatacre himself, worked harder than anyone else. He had no tent, only a waterproof sheet like the rest of the men, and shared with them equally all the exposure and fatigue of the march. His energy was inexhaustible, and he allowed no detail to escape him, for though he made the men work hard, he was careful of their comfort in many little ways. He saw that they had fresh instead of tinned meat whenever it was possible to obtain it, and always tried to arrange for it to be cooked at the time when it was to be eaten, so that they might have it hot, with all its juice, and get as much good out of it as possible. These little matters are of more importance than they seem. Moltke said that the first part of an army to wear out is its feet, but it is a question whether its stomach is not quite as vulnerable.

As soon as the troops reached Ashreth heliographic communication was established from the crest of the pass with Gujar on the one side and Ashreth on the other; the helio messages being flashed to the top of a hill just above Ashreth, and transmitted to the camp by flag signals. The signallers had hard, trying work all through the campaign. They had to stand for hours at the signal station at the top of the pass in an icy cold wind, and in other places suffered almost as much from exposure to the sun.

The use made of the telegraph in so mountainous and difficult a country, and the speed with which it was brought up behind the troops was a very noticeable feature of the march. It was brought into Chitral within two days from the arrival there of the 3rd Brigade; a wonderful achievement when the nature of the ground over which it had to pass is taken into consideration. What the ground was like may be judged from this photograph, showing the construction of the telegraph on the Dir side of the Lowarai Pass. On good ground a mile of wire could be put up in an hour, but over mountain passes the rate of progress was of course considerably slower. It is a fact worth recording that on the morning of the 13th of April the telegraph office in the camp at Sado was put into direct communication with the telegraph office at Simla, and Sir Robert Low had a conference of more than an hour with the commander-in-chief. Sir George White, though they were separated by two chains of mountains, and by a distance of more than six hundred miles.

General Gatacre received orders to halt at Ashreth, and was detained there for some time, but the day after it was reached Major "Roddy" Owen, of the Lancashire Fusiliers, who was corresponding for the *Pioneer*, and Captain Younghusband, the *Times* correspondent, rode on by themselves to Chitral, a distance of thirty-eight miles. It

VILLAGE BETWEEN DIR AND GUJAR

BRIDGE BETWEEN ZIARAT AND ASHRETH.

was a very plucky thing to do, for the siege had only just been raised, and the country was in a most unsettled state.

The road, too, was very bad. Indeed, until the sappers took it in hand, in one or two places where it crosses the face of a precipitous cliff, it was almost impracticable for mules. Altogether it was a most hazardous ride.

After about a fortnight's delay General Gatacre moved on to Chitral, Sir Robert Low and the headquarters staff following a day or two later. On his arrival there on the 16th May, Sir Robert Low reviewed all the troops then in Chitral: the Gilgit Relief Force, the 3rd Brigade of the Chitral Relief Force, and the half company of the 14th Sikhs, who had been in fort during the siege, looking haggard and weak after their long fast, but with the proud bearing of men who have fought a good fight and won it. The rest of the garrison, the 4th Kashmir Rifles, had been sent with Whitchurch to escort Campbell and the sick convoy to Gilgit. It was a grandly dramatic spectacle. The little *mehtar*, Shuja-ul-Mulk, was introduced to Sir Robert Low by Mr. Robertson, who wore his arm in a sling, for he was still suffering from his wound. A salute of thirteen guns was fired, which immensely impressed the crowd of Chitralis who were looking on, and Sir Robert Low briefly addressed the troops.

The morning was a lovely one, calm and cloudless, and Chitral, beautiful at all times, never looked more beautiful than it did then. The troops were drawn up on the slope of the hill between the bridge and the village of Danin. Behind them rose the giant peaks of Tiritch Mir. Immediately beneath them flowed the river, with the fort on the opposite bank, dismantled and gory from the fierce struggle through which it had passed. Beyond it stretched the valley, green with fruit-trees and waving cornfields. Sher Afzul's house could be seen on the crest of the hill to the right, and to the left the house of Rab Nawaz Khan could just be discerned through the thicket of trees that surrounded it; while Rab Nawaz Khan himself was present, terribly slashed about, and with one arm disabled forever, but looking full of life and energy still.

On May 18th Sir Robert Low and his staff left Chitral again for Dir, and on the 19th Mr. Robertson and Colonel Durand, the Military Secretary to the Viceroy, started for India by way of Swat and Jandol, it being thought advisable that Mr. Robertson should see that route. It must have seemed strange to Colonel Durand, who had visited the old *mehtar* Aman-ul-Mulk in Chitral in 1888, at a time when

DIR VALLEY SHOWING TELEGRAPH IN PROCESS OF CONSTRUCTION

FIELD TELEGRAPH OFFICE, SADO

the only other Englishmen who had set foot there were Major Bid-dulph and Sir William Lockhart, to see the Buffs and the Highlanders walking unconcernedly about the valley. Mr. Robertson took with him to India Sipat Bahadur and Morad Khan, the two Gilgiti chief-tains who did such splendid service during the siege, and before he went he bade farewell to Gurmokh Singh and the 14th Sikhs in a few dignified and touching words. Harley marched them down to Mardan about a month later, but of the company of 200 men who had been detached from the regiment only two years before for service in the Gilgit agency, only 110 went back. The rest had died or been killed.

Before Mr. Robertson went away the Government had decided that Amir-ul-Mulk could not be allowed to remain in Chitral with safety to Shuja-ul-Mulk, so he was taken down in custody to Mardan by the provost-marshal, Captain W. F. Shakespear of the 6th Bengal Cavalry. He had been in custody ever since the beginning of the siege, and was now formally handed over by Gurdon to Shakespear and an escort of the Buffs. A number of Chitralis were looking on, but not one of them showed the slightest sign either of sympathy or of respect. It was a curious reversal of fortune, Gurdon delivering over as a pris-oner the man in whose power he had been for so long.

When he reached Dir, Shakespear was provided with an escort of the Guides Cavalry, and proceeded rapidly to Mardan, which was reached on the seventh day after leaving Chitral. There he handed over Amir-ul-Mulk to the civil authorities, and he is now in custody at Dharmsala with Sher Afzul and Yadgar Beg and the other Chitrali prisoners.

VIEW IN CHITRAL VALLEY.

CHAPTER 18

Transport Difficulties

It was not until the 16th March that the Government of India gave final orders for the mobilisation of the 1st Division. The troops were ordered to concentrate at Nowshera, the railway base, on the 26th March, and to advance on the 28th; and in spite of the heavy rains which cut up the roads and caused serious delay these orders were duly carried out.

It was the first occasion that had presented itself for testing the new army mobilisation scheme, and Major-General Stedman, the quartermaster-general in India, Colonel E. R. Ellis, and Captain Kemball, the three officers on whom the chief responsibility rested of putting it into practical working, are to be congratulated on its entire success.

How great the transport and commissariat difficulties alone were, may be imagined from the number of animals employed. On the 2nd of May there were more than 35,000 pack animals at work, 10,000 only being on the permanent strength of the division. Rather over 25,000 had to be bought hurriedly and sent up as rapidly as possible to the front. The exact numbers are—camels hired 6,845 r purchased 1,003; mules hired 3,519; purchased 534; bullocks hired 7,329; donkeys hired 2,718; purchased 198; ponies purchased 3,026; total 25,172. Besides these the elephants belonging to the Campbellpore elephant battery were made use of to take up the twelve pontoons for the permanent bridge over the Swat River. That pontoons should be able to be sent across the Malakand Pass at all says a great deal for the excellence of the road made over it by Major Abbot, R.E.

The elephants were a great source of wonderment to the Swatis, who had never seen any before. One of the officers of the 1st Brigade one afternoon, when there was no work for them to do, amused himself by taking them over to a Swati village and giving the children rides upon their backs. A travelled graybeard who was there kept saying to the other villagers, "I told you I had seen an animal in India with a long nose; you wouldn't believe me, but here it is."

It should be remembered to the credit of the railway authorities, who, as a rule, come in for much undeserved reviling on account of unavoidable delays, that their organisation stood the unusual strain so well that in spite of the congestion of traffic caused by the despatch to Nowshera of so many animals, and of such enormous quantities of supplies, it was never found necessary to suspend the ordinary passenger traffic between Lahore and Peshawur.

One of the minor difficulties the transport officers had to contend with was the shipment of camels. They had never before been railed in large numbers, and it was anticipated that they would give much trouble; but these fears fortunately proved groundless. They were made to kneel down in open trucks—four in each truck, with a camel driver to look after them, and presented a very comical appearance with "their ugly heads a-bobbing like a bucket full of snakes."

It was difficult to obtain as many animals as were required for so large a force in the short time allowed for mobilisation, and the Imperial Service Transport trains volunteered by the *Maharajahs* of Gwalior and Jeypore were of signal service all through the campaign. Both these corps are maintained in a complete state of readiness for war, and the rapidity with which they mobilised was remarkable. The Gwalior corps, which was raised in 1891, left Gwalior within two days from the time when it was warned for service, and joined the Chitral Relief Force at Nowshera on April 1st with 456 ponies and 193 transport carts. Captain Edwards of the Central India Horse, inspecting officer of the Central India Imperial Service Cavalry and Transport, who has had a great deal to do with the corps ever since it was raised, being attached to it for duty. It should be mentioned that in addition to this corps H.H. the Maharajah Sindia of Gwalior also maintains for Imperial defence two regiments of lancers, each six hundred strong.

The Jeypore Corps was raised between 1889 and 1891 by the present Maharajah H.H. Sawai Madho Singh, G.C.S.I., who chose to forego the prestige and *éclat* attaching to the possession of combatant troops in order to contribute what he believed to be a more useful and necessary assistance to Imperial defence in the shape of a transport train. He has always taken the keenest personal interest in it, inspecting it himself at regular intervals and sparing no expense to maintain it in the highest efficiency. The lines he has had made for it in Jeypore

CAMP, JELLALA, LOOKING NORTH

CAMP, JELLALA, LOOKING SOUTH

were designed by Colonel Jacob R.E., C.I.E., the superintending engineer of the Jeypore State, and are the most complete of their kind in India.

The corps is composed of a thousand ponies and four hundred carts, the equipment being alternative and available for use either in draught or pack, for though it is primarily a cart train, it has also been carefully trained in pack work. It is always kept maintained complete in every particular, with hospitals, veterinary establishment, and workshop, in which its own equipment is manufactured as well as repairs effected. It is divided into six troops of 150 ponies and there is also a training depot of 100 ponies.

The corps was warned for service on the 26th March, and left Jeypore within forty-eight hours, in six special trains, each train containing a troop with its ponies, carts, equipment, and repairing establishment. At first it was employed as a cart train between Jellala and Dargai, but later on during the campaign it was sent up to Dir, ninety miles distant, with provisions for the Chitral garrison, which it put down at Dir in seven days without the loss of a single bag or of a single pony. When I saw the corps in Nowshera at the end of June, the ponies, though they had had three months' continuous work, were looking hard and fit, and there was scarcely a sick one amongst them. The Maharajah of Jeypore is indeed to be congratulated on the possession of so splendid a corps, and the greatest credit is due to the superintendent, Rai Dhanpat Raie Rai Bahadur, to Captain Tate, of the 15th Bengal Lancers, the inspecting officer of the Imperial Service Cavalry and Transport in Rajputana and the North-West Provinces, who has been closely connected with the corps ever since its formation, and to Lieutenant Munn, of the 36th Sikhs, who, as well as Captain Tate, was with it during the campaign.

I have described these two corps rather in detail, not only because their remarkable efficiency is in itself noteworthy, but because they belong to the Imperial Service troops, which were only raised a few years ago, and which have not been employed before on active service. It is exceedingly satisfactory to find that they can do such excellent work, and it would seem to point to the conclusion that in our wars of the future in India, the Imperial Service troops will play an important part. It must be remembered that with the exception of the 14th Sikhs, the troops who held Chitral Fort were Kashmir Imperial Service troops.

In estimating the difficulties which the transport and commissariat had to surmount it must be borne in mind that the country through which the force had to proceed was entirely unknown, and that until the sappers and miners and the pioneers had been at work on them the roads were mere mountain tracks, not difficult or dangerous as they are in Chitral, but tedious and easily blocked. After a time, when Major Abbot had finished his road over the Malakand, and there were bridges over both the Swat and Panjkora Rivers, everything worked smoothly enough, and the sending up of supplies to the front was a comparatively easy matter; but at the outset the difficulties were very great, and the transport and commissariat officers had great exposure and exceedingly hard work.

It was not only the men who had to be fed, but the animals also. The valleys in Dir and Chitral, though exceedingly fertile, are narrow and confined, and could not long supply even grass for the mules, so compressed fodder had to be sent up for them from India. But in spite of bad roads and bad weather both departments stood the test excellently, and there was never a dearth of food either for man or beast. One of the men put it very tersely. He was heard to say: "Well, I can't say I've anything to complain about. My father used to tell me that he had to fight on an empty stomach, and I've always had plenty of food during this show."

KHAR VALLEY CAMELS COMING DOWN THE
MALAKAND PASS, AND VILLAGE OF KHAR
BURNING IN THE DISTANCE.

CHAPTER 19

Umra Khan

Umra Khan was born about 1860, and is the fifth of the six sons of Aman Khan of Jandol, who died in 1879, and was succeeded by his eldest son.

The new *khan*, not—as was afterwards shown—without reason, grew afraid of the turbulent and restless disposition of his younger brother, and Umra Khan had to take refuge in flight. Finding himself friendless and homeless, he went on a pilgrimage to Mecca. He came back in 1881, stole a rifle in Peshawur from the lines of one of the regiments stationed there, and made his way secretly to Jandol. There he was joined by half a dozen men who were willing to link their fortunes to his, and dressing them and himself in women's clothes he waited one morning outside the walls of the fort at Barwa. When the *khan* came out, seeing as he thought only a group of women, he had no suspicion of danger, and Umra Khan was able to approach quite close, and to shoot him dead with the rifle he carried concealed in his woman's dress. He then entered the fort with his followers, and barricaded himself securely in one of the upper rooms.

For some days all was confusion in Jandol, no man daring to do anything for fear of compromising himself. Then the old queen stood out upon the wall of the fort, and addressed the people. "O men of Jandol," she said "why are you troubled? Is it not sufficient for you that one of my sons shall reign over you? Surely it is for them to decide amongst themselves which it shall be. *That* is no concern of yours!"

This speech seemed a reasonable one to those who heard it, and encouraged by the applause which greeted it, Umra Khan came forward, and, binding the *pugaree*, the emblem of rule, around his head, became *Khan* of Jandol in the place of his brother. He did not injure his other brothers. To three of them he gave villages, and the youngest

161

UPPER KOLUNDAI VILLAGE, NEAR GUJAR

of all, Mahomed Shah, he subsequently made *Khan* of Dir.

His first care after his accession was to obtain as many rifles as he could, and to raise a little band of men upon whom he could depend. Before long he had nearly a hundred well-paid, well-drilled men, among them being many deserters from Indian regiments, armed with Martinis and Sniders. He also raised a small troop of horse about eighty in number. They were the only cavalry in Swat or Bajour, and proved of great service to him, for all these hill tribes have a great dread of cavalry.

As soon as he had enlisted enough men he began to make incursions into the neighbouring states. His first war was with Mahomed Sharif the Khan of Dir, the hereditary chief of the Yusufzais, who are by far the most important of the Pathan tribes. He allied himself with Mian Gul, a son of the famous *Akhoond*, the priest-ruler of Swat, and their combined forces succeeded in defeating the far larger army of Dir. Mahomed Sharif was obliged to submit, and lost a large slice of the Baraul valley. I came across an old iron-worker in a hamlet a few miles out of Dir on the way to the Lowarai Pass, whose body is warped and twisted with the wounds he received when fighting for Mahomed Sharif during this war. It is extraordinary that he ever survived them.

The tenure by which most of the land is held in Dir and Jandol is very similar to the ancient feudal tenure of Europe. The tribesmen are all free Pathans, not slaves like so many of the Chitralis, and their chiefs like the Norman lord, is merely *primus inter pares*. They pay no rent for their land, but they have to render homage to their *khan* upon his accession, and if he goes to war one member of each household must go with him. An old *lumberdar* in the Janbatai valley explained it to me thus: "When the summons comes, taking with me my sword and blanket, I must go forth to fight for my *khan*, the *Khan* of Dir."

Some years ago I went across to Ranighat, in the territory of the Khuda Kheyls. It was harvest time, and as we were riding along I noticed that every villager as he worked in his field was armed with sword and gun, which he kept handy by him, if not actually carrying them. I asked my guide—one of their headmen—"Who is chief over you?" and he replied, "We have none—we are all equal."

"How then," I asked, "do you administer justice?"

"We each avenge our own wrongs," was the grim reply.

After peace had been declared and Mian Gul had withdrawn his men to Swat, Umra Khan treacherously turned round and made an alliance with the defeated Mahomed Sharif, and they together attacked and defeated Mian Gul. A few years after, in 1890, in alliance with the *Khan* of Asmar, and Safdar Khan of Nawagai, he again attacked Mahomed Sharif, expelled him from Dir, and made his brother, Mahomed Shah, *Khan* of Dir in his stead. After that he turned his attention to Asmar, which he invaded and subdued. Asmar, however, is under the protection of the *amir*, one of whose sons has married a sister of the *khan*, and the *amir* could not brook any interference in that quarter. Umra Khan had to withdraw his troops, having incurred the lasting enmity of the *amir*, an enmity likely to prove of consequence to him now that he is in his power, for the *amir* is not a man who forgets.

Being thwarted in Asmar, he then found a pretext to quarrel with Swat, and, in June, 1893, advanced against the Dosha Kheyls, one of the tribes of Swat, killed about a hundred of their men, and seized 7,000 head of cattle, in retaliation, as he said, for the murder of two of his servants by the Dosha Kheyls. He took the opportunity at the same time to again subdue Barangola and Badiya, two chief villages in Swat, which had formerly submitted to him, but had recently revolted.

These incursions thoroughly alarmed the Swatis, and they appealed to the Government of India for help. It was not thought advisable to become entangled in these petty frontier squabbles, so the Swatis were told that we could not interfere. Umra Khan, however, was warned that he must abstain from harassing his neighbours. Though he had begun his reign as *khan* only of the little valley of Jandol, he had by this time established his authority over all Bajour (with the exception of Asmar), and his influence was great amongst the wild tribes of Swat, Boner, and Yaghistan; while his standard, a white triangular banner with a blood-red hand, was feared by all of them. He had also established a reputation for sanctity, and had led several religious raids or "*jehads*" against the idolaters of Kafiristan. One of his wives was a daughter of the old *mehtar* Aman-ul-Mulk, and a sister both of Amir-ul-Mulk, and of the present *mehtar* Shuja-ul-Mulk. This gave him a pretext for interference in the internal intrigues of Chitral, and it is believed that the assassination of Nizam-ul-Mulk was instigated by him.

When the English troops took possession of Jandol he fled to Kabul, where he was at first kindly received, though it is said that he has since been thrown into prison. He behaved with such generosity to Edwardes and Fowler, and prevented so much useless bloodshed by his discretion in avoiding a hopeless conflict with the overwhelming force sent against him, that it is sincerely to be hoped that measures will be taken to secure his release unharmed, even though it may be deemed inexpedient to give him back Jandol.

Before this expedition the Jandolis were generally thought to be a very fanatical race,—a most mistaken estimate. Umra Khan never even hinted that Edwardes or Fowler should become Mussulmans, and though the three Hindu *sepoys* who were with them were told that they must learn the *"Kalimah"* or profession of faith—*"Bismillah. Hir ech man! Mir Rahim! Ha! Illah!! Illallah!!! Ho Mahomet des Rasullulah!"*—they were never troubled in any other way on account of their religion. Indeed there is so little fanaticism that many Hindu traders live there permanently. These traders were most anxious to supply anything they might require to Edwardes and Fowler, who accordingly had clothes made for themselves and their *sepoys*, merely giving a receipt for the amount.

The men dress in the same way as all other Pathans. They wear a white or blue skull cap, with a white or blue cotton *pugaree* wound around it, a white shirt, and a loose embroidered waistcoat, worn un-buttoned, very loose flowing pyjamas, and green shoes with turned up toes.

There is very little *"purdah"* or concealment of the women, who go about with uncovered faces, and mingle freely with the men, laughing and chatting with them quite concernedly. They wear very few ornaments; but in one of the houses in Miankalai, the chief village in Jandol, I found some strings of beads, a very prettily shaped pair of scissors, and some painted slicks which they use for putting *surma* or antimony on to the eyes. I was amused also to find nailed up against the wall a sheet from the *Lady's Pictorial*.

A man's chief ornaments are his gun and *bandolier* and belt full of cartridges. The gun is always loaded and carried in the hand ready for instant use, for blood feuds are very common. Their talk, too, amongst themselves is generally about guns. Their own are matchlocks, but they have stolen a good many Martinis and Sniders from the Indian government.

Umra Khan was conspicuous in that he was the only man who went about unarmed. He did not observe much state, and anyone could come up to him, and prefer a petition or complaint; but he was always attended by a guard—a very necessary precaution. He is a tall man, with powerful arms and chest, but with rather round shoulders. Like most Pathans he has his head clean shaved. His face is long and

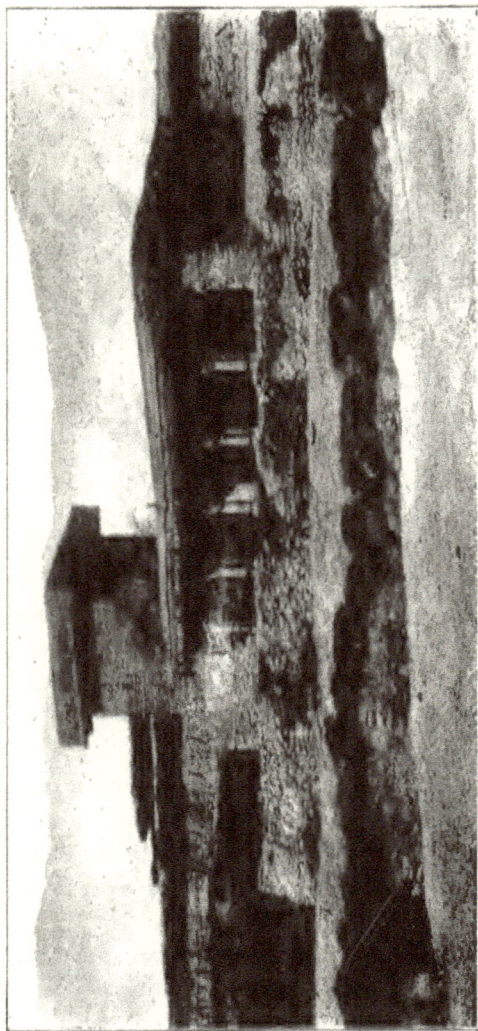

Umra Khan's mosque, in Fort Mundar

thin, with a big nose and strong firm mouth. He dresses well and cleanly, but quietly and without ostentation, not like his brother Mahomed Shah, who is a great dandy, delighting in gaily embroidered waistcoats. He does not approve of smoking.

Though not a fanatic, he is very sincerely religious. He is a diligent student of the *Koran*, and prays long and often. He never fails to put on clean clothes at sunset to pray in. One day, when on the way across the Lowarai Pass, he said to the two officers, "It you want to have a quiet time in which to say your prayers, you can say them in a corner of the mosque when I say mine." He does not speak Hindustani, only Pushtu and Persian.

On the whole he was popular with the Jandolis, for he was a strong man who kept them from being raided; but he had many enemies, principally men whose land he had seized to give to his imported *sepoys*. He has several wives, and a good many children. One of his principal amusements is hawking, most of his hawks being imported from Chitral, where they are particularly fine. I was shown a beautiful peregrine at Mastuj, which had been found sitting quietly outside one of the houses in the village of Sanoghar, after the fight at Nisa Gol. His habits are extremely frugal, and when on the march he is most abstemious, his food being only boiled rice and a little soup. When at home he lived rather better, but even then not in any way luxuriously; a big wooden dish, about three feet in diameter, being heaped up with boiled rice and placed in the centre of the room.

Round this were placed little plates of cream, honey, milk, and curds. There was also a bucket full of Pathan bread, and a large dish of greens, and of soup with meat in it. After he had washed his hands the *khan* helped himself to one of the side dishes. His companions, of whom there were often as many as fifteen or twenty, then did the same. A little was taken with the fingers from the mound of rice in the centre and dipped into a side dish, and the morsel was then popped neatly into the mouth—a feat the English officers say they found very difficult to accomplish until they had had some practice. It recalls Chaucer's description of the *prioresse*, Madame Eglentyne.

> *At meté wel y-taught was she with-alle,*
> *She leet no morsel from her lippes falle,*
> *Ne wette her fingrés in hir saucé depe.*
> *Wel coude she carie a morsel and wel kepe*
> *That no drope ne fille upon hire breste.*

When the meal—which only lasted about ten minutes—was over, there was a general washing of hands.

Edwardes gives the following interesting account in his diary of their life in Jandol:—

Umra Khan always gave orders to give us the best food obtainable, and it was not his fault if his servants did not always carry out his instructions. On the march we did not get much, because it was not to be had, but when obtainable, until panic set in among the people at the approach of our troops, we were supplied with two fowls, *atta*, rice, *ghi*, and milk each day.

From Chitral Fort we had got blankets, plates, etc., also a bag of sugar and a pound of tea, which were great luxuries. We cooked our food with the assistance of our *sepoys*. The *sepoy* prisoners were given the same food as Umra Khan's own men; on the march the ration was very small. We were never in any way threatened, but we knew we were always liable to be killed by some fanatic who had a blood feud against our people. Our strong guard, armed always with loaded rifles, who never for a moment allowed us more than a few yards from them, were doubtless as much for our protection as to prevent our escape. We were not allowed to communicate with anyone except through the *khan*, nor were we allowed writing materials. We got some paper and a pencil in Chitral, and kept a short diary of each day hid in our clothes.

The three Hindu *sepoy* prisoners were made to learn the *Kalim*, and their hair was cut, but they were not made to publicly declare themselves Mussulmans, and they never really became so. We officers were never in any way asked to become Mussulmans, nor did there appear to be any fanatical feeling against us by the people we met. They would eat our bread and give us theirs. We were continually asked how we existed without *sharab*, and in Chitral were offered the contents of all the medicine bottles taken in the hospital outside the fort as a substitute. This we declined. We were naturally an object of great curiosity, and crowds came to see us. They specially delighted to see us eat with knife and fork, or attempt to eat with our fingers. This was often annoying, and our guard soon understood we did not like visitors at meal times.

At other times we received the public and sat to be inspected, conversation being carried on under difficulties. Umra Khan himself always treated us civilly, was much interested in what we said, and when he was with us and had leisure sent for us each day. He twice took us out hawking quail, and asked us to walk with him.

With the exception of the letters mentioned in our report, sent through Umra Khan, we were allowed no materials for writing, and some paper we had caused to be purchased at Barwa was seized, and the *bania* fined. We were allowed to purchase materials to make clothes for ourselves and our *sepoys*; the *banias* gave us credit on our written acknowledgment.

When we went to Mandia we were smuggled into the fort there after dark; and after Edwardes had left, Fowler had an anxious time, owing to the presence of many fanatics from outside gaining entrance into the fort. There was very nearly a fight between them and Umra Khan's men inside the fort on the 15th April. Umra Khan gave Edwardes back his own sword, looted at Reshun, which Umra Khan had received as a present from Chitral, and promised to obtain Fowler's for him, if it could be found. We both consider that Umra Khan treated us very well indeed, and that he never intended to be the direct cause of any injury to us under any circumstances.

ZIARAT, LOWARAI PASS.

LOWARAI PASS: VIEW FROM GUJAR LOOKING SOUTH

CHAPTER 20

Chitrali Customs

The Chitralis are a merry, lively people, with exceedingly pleasant, frank, open faces. Their houses are rather dirty, but they are not in themselves like the Dir people, who are so dirty that a native officer, a Pathan—and the Pathans are not a very cleanly people—writing to one of his officers in India, said: "These people are the dirtiest I have ever seen. They are more like beasts than men." The Chitralis, though not scrupulously clean according to European ideas, are not dirty to that extent. They are great swimmers, and will jump without hesitation into the swiftest current. I saw a man swim across the Yarkun River near Kogazai, where the stream is very strong. They generally make use of an inflated skin, carrying it with them uninflated, and inflating it when required. If they did not do this they would often find themselves unable to get back to their homes, for the rivers in Chitral rise very suddenly, and come down with great violence. They are keen sportsmen, good shots, and bold riders, thinking nothing of swimming a horse across a swollen torrent. Once when Aman-ul-Mulk was out hawking and his favourite hawk flew over the Chitral River, which was in flood at the time, and could not be induced to come back, Asfandiar, one of his sons, plunged in with his horse, and brought it across with him, pleasing the old man so much that he gave him the exclusive right of shooting and hawking in a particularly good ravine near the Chitral fort, reserving only the right to shoot or hawk there himself if he wished to do so.

The ponies are small and generally under-fed, but they are exceedingly wiry, and can go great distances; and the Chitralis play polo on them for hours at a time. Polo is the national game, every village having a polo-ground. The village band is always in attendance, and plays furiously during the exciting moments of the game. After it is over there is tea and dancing, the losing side having to dance.

One evening Mr. Robertson very kindly arranged a concert for us in the courtyard of Sher Afzul's house, the principal drummer being a Puniali boy who was outside the fort during the siege, and who used to play constantly in the summer-house to drown the noise of the mining. The Punialis in the fort declare that he tried to warn them by calling out in Puniali "*dar*," "*dar*," "attack," "attack," as he drummed; but it is hardly likely that he would have dared to do it, for if any of the bystanders had happened to understand Puniali they would certainly have cut his throat. It was probably only the rhythmical chant the drummers all use when drumming. But the Punialis believed firmly that he had tried to give them notice of the attack, and he was naturally a great favourite. After the dancing, several Chitrali songs were sung. The airs are rather pretty, with a good deal of wild melody, and not at all like the monotonous nasal drone of the Hindustani songs. The singers sat on the ground, huddled up close to each other, and bobbed their heads in unison in a very ridiculous way.

The flowers in Chitral are lovely, and the people are very fond of decking themselves with them. When we first arrived, the valleys were filled with the fragrance of a most delicious yellow flower called, I believe, the *eleagnus*. Unfortunately, it only lasted for a very few days. The Chitralis wound great sprays of it round their woollen caps. The roses, too, were exquisite, and so were the pomegranates, with their deep red, odourless flowers. They, and the roses, and the wild vine grew festooned together in the most beautiful way imaginable. On the Lowarai Pass we found a good deal of honeysuckle and a quaintly pretty prickly little yellow flower, from which the natives told me they make a medicine for the eyes. All over these hills, from Swat right through to Kashmir, there are great numbers of mulberry trees; and in Chitral there are plum, peach, apricot, and cherry-trees as well, and quantities of vines. The Chitralis, being Mahommedans, do not make wine, but they make quantities of raisins, and are as fond of grapes as the Pathans, who have a saying, "Who has not tasted Cabul grapes thinks wild sloes very fine."

The grapes in Kafiristan are said to be particularly luscious, and the Kafirs make wine out of them, but it is not particularly nice. An old Kafir, with a great admiration for Mr. Robertson, whom he had known during his adventurous stay in Kafiristan, brought him a skinful of it, and we all tasted it, but very few of us cared to do so again. It was a light white wine, a kind of natural hock—just the pure juice

LOWARAI PASS

VIEW IN THE CHITRAL VALLEY BETWEEN ASHRETH
AND KILA DROSH

of the grape—and would probably have been very good if it had not been tainted by the curious musty smell which clings to everything that a Kafir has, and which is probably due to peat smoke.

The bulk of the Chitralis are slaves, belonging absolutely to the *adamzadas* or nobles. They can be sold anywhere in Chitral, but not out of Chitral, except by the permission of the *mehtar.* The common people would gladly welcome British influence, but the *adamzadas* would naturally resist it. It was known all over the Hindu Khush that we had procured the release of a number of slaves from the Chinese upon the Pamirs, amongst them being a good many Chitralis, and it was believed that we always try to abolish slavery wherever we go, and that we would probably do so in Chitral.

I had a long talk with a man in Yasin, and he told me that the people there had been quite happy and contented since the English had come. I asked him why. He said, "Because the *rajah* is no longer allowed to seize and carry away my wife or daughter, or to plunder me of all my crops as he used to do." It is, however, a comparatively easy matter to restrain the nobles from committing acts of oppression. It would be a very difficult one to bring about the abolition of slavery altogether, for, the land being entirely in the hands of the nobles, the slaves would starve if suddenly freed. It is a question that may safely be left to Mr. Robertson to deal with. It existed in an even more acute form in Hunza-Nagar, and if he has been able to make the people there contented and prosperous, he may be trusted to bring about the same happy result in Chitral.

Although they are Mahommedans the Chitralis are very fond of dogs. When Sir William Lockhart visited, the country in 1886 he gave the *mehtar* a white bulldog. Surgeon-Captain Luard found this dog wandering about in the village of Kogazai, and took it back with him to Gilgit. He seemed very glad to get back again amongst the *sahibs* after his long exile of nine years. Quite a number of dogs distinguished themselves during the campaign. Harley had a big yellow pariah dog, called Ghazi, with him in the fort, who was a great favourite with all of them. He was hit three times, but without being much damaged. The third time he was hit in the foot, which festered, and after the siege was over it became necessary to destroy him. Edwardes had a little fox-terrier with him at Reshun, who was shot through the chest, but not very badly injured.

The Pathans allowed him to take her down to Jandol, and she was with him when he was sent by Umra Khan into General Low's camp, and became a great pet in the 2nd Brigade. Then there was a pariah dog who atthed himself to the Buffs at Chakdara in the Swat Vallev, and marched all the way with them to Chitral; and another who joined the Gordons, or the King's Own Scottish Borderers—I forget which—at Dargai, and went up with them to the assault on the Malakand. He was greatly interested in the Guides fight on the Panjkora, and swam across the river to their camp, coming back after a bit on one of the rafts.

The language spoken by the Chitralis is called Khowar. It is quite a distinct language, and has no affinity whatever with Pushtu, the language of the Afghans. The only Englishman who can talk it, I believe—with the exception of Major Biddulph—is Captain O'Brien, of the 15th Sikhs, who was stationed in Chitral for a year as the officer in command of the political officer's escort. He made a special study of it, and has lately published a Chitrali grammar. He very kindly obtained for me the words of some Chitrali songs, of which I have made a translation. They are all love songs.

I tried hard to get some war songs as well, but the Chitralis assured us that they had none, that they had only love songs; and this I believe must be the case, for Captain Townshend told me that when the musicians were playing in the summer-house during the construction of the mine, they kept continually singing the first of the songs I have translated, which is a particularly sentimental love song. I have given the Chitrali words also, in order to show the metre. I have not, of course, translated each word literally, but I have given faithfully the spirit of the song.

O sweetheart of mine, I am worn to a shade
By the yearning the glow of thy beauty hath made.
Dear eyes of my soul, wilt thou still look askance
On me, far too low for the boon of thy glance?

In thy home thou'rt a treasure, an oriole outside;
Of thy love who can measure the joy and the pride?
The mere fragrance thereof hath bereft me of sense,
And I think of nought else when thou sendest me hence.

For ah, my sweet starling, my love is so keen.
That could my arms once round thy dear neck have been,
That is whiter than milk, thou should'st ne'er hear a sigh
Of regret if thereafter they doom me to die.

NATIVE HOUSE NEAR GUJAR ON THE WAY
TO THE LOWARAI PASS

The starling is the myna or Indian starling, of which there are numbers in Chitral. There are also a great many golden *orioles*—a beautiful bird with exquisite plumage, and a sweet, full note.

The Chitrali words, it will be seen, have a very distinct and regular metre. They are these:

Ta nang oché namoos
Cheké ma marisana,
Tan herdi-o-ghichen
Fakir-o-noh lolisana.

Bulbul doori asur
Maiyun beri rem,
Ta ash, k-o-wori mati giti
Dak gaderi rem.

Hai, hai ma bulbul
Ma shariki rem,
Chingoli chakoom hai rafigh
Ma mariki rem.

They are a very superstitious people, and believe firmly in fairies and elves, and good and evil spirits. This is shown in the following song:

There are fairies everywhere,
On the earth and in the air;
Working weal and working woe,
Myriad fairy creatures go.

When antimony adorns thine eyes,
look not into the skies;
Should some fairy being see
He will sure thy lover be.

Though thy mother scowl with hate,
I reck neither her nor fate;
Thou alone my joy can be,
Thou, the heart of life to me.

     Refrain.

Then abide with me here, sweet, no more let us roam,
Thou shalt dwell in a garden, ever fragrant in flower;
When the snow lieth deep on our cool mountain home,
In the warm vale beneath I will build thee a bower.

O daughter of Mirza, with falcon-like eyes.
Thou art whiter than milk, thou art chaster than ice.

I was only able to obtain one other song, a dance lilt. The Chitrali women, I should mention, wear their hair in a low fringe over the forehead.

In the springtime, in the springtime
When the leaves and grass are green,
With thy black fringe o'er thy forehead
Thou, my little love, art seen;

Singing gaily like a bulbul,
Like a myna clear and true.
Ah, why don't they give thee to me,
Without thee what can I do?

For I love thee, yea I love thee,
More than country, more than life,
And I'd work for thee for ever
If they'd give me thee for wife;
For thou singest like a bulbul.
Like a myna clear and true;
Love, I cannot live without thee,
Love, dear love, what shall I do?

I give below the literal rendering of two of the songs; I have unfortunately mislaid that of the third. It will be seen that I have kept to the originals fairly closely.

(1)

Fairies are passing, passing to work good or mischief, sweet- heart, should you look up you will see a fairy boy above you, ready for your love. You please your lover with your eyes blacked with antimony. If I enter your house your mother eyes me with hatred^ but I care for no one but you, you are my life's joy.

Refrain.

Come to me, dear, come my love,
Let me take you into the garden,
When the mountains are snowbound
I will take you to the warm valleys,
O daughter of Mirza with falcon's eyes,
Chaste maiden whiter than milk.

178

(2)

In the springtime when all is green
You are my sweet maid, you are
My little myna bird, my little bulbul,
Your black fringe reaches to your eyebrows.
Oh, what shall I do?
Why don't they give thee to me,
Oh, what shall I do?

You are dearer to me than life, sweetheart,
You are as dear as country and home,
Indeed you are far dearer;
I am ready to work for you forever.
Oh, what shall I do?
Why don't they give thee to me,
Oh, what shall I do?

CHAPTER 21

Probable March of Alexander
the Great

We first met the Kafirs when we were encamped at Girzar on the top of the Lowarai Pass. Five or six wild-looking men came into camp there, whom we found to be Kafirs from the other side of the Kunar River. One of them spoke a little broken Pushtu and acted as interpreter.

Very little is yet known of their country. Sir William Lockhart went a few miles across the border from Chitral, but that was all, and Colonel Holdich in the spring of the present year penetrated a little way into it from Asmar with a strong escort from the Afghan Delimitation Commission.

The little information we had about it before that was obtained by Colonel Tanner and Major Biddulph. But a year or two ago Sir George Robertson went right into the interior and stayed for more than eight months in Kandesh, the principal village in the country. He made a careful study of the customs and language of the people, and his report, which the Government of India are about to publish for general information, will be of fascinating interest.

They are a queer, wild-looking race, very dirty and unkempt, but with a certain little grace of movement and figure. They are called "*Kafirs*" or idolaters by their Mahommedan neighbours, for whom they cherish an implacable hatred; not without just cause, for they are continually making forays into their country and carrying off their women and children.

The women are said to be very beautiful; indeed the Afghans have a saying that the most valuable possessions a man can have are a Baluch mare and a Kafiristani slave girl. The Kafirs naturally retaliate, but

180

they are handicapped for want of proper weapons. They have only bows and arrows, which they use with great precision, and daggers, which are of a very peculiar and distinctive shape, with a cross-shaped iron hilt, studded with brass nails. They carry them in a triangular iron sheath slung in a belt of untanned leather. I succeeded in getting one, which remains in my possession.

Wood mentions that in 1838 he found the valley of the Upper Kokcha deserted on account of the Kafir forays. But their favourite hunting ground is the Lowarai Pass. There they lie in wait for solitary travellers, and come upon them suddenly unawares, or kill them when asleep. One gloomy defile in the pass is full of the graves of the victims, called by the Mahommedans "The Tombs of the Martyrs."

There was an old Kafir with rather a handsome face, but with the odour of Esau, who used constantly to come into Chitral to see Mr. Robertson, for whom he had a great regard. He was one of the richest and most influential men in Kafiristan, and had killed more than a hundred Mahommedans with his own hand. He explained to me very vividly in dumb show—for we could neither of us speak the other's language—his method of attack: a sleeping man, a stealthy approach from behind, and a sudden stab with the dagger just over the heart. When they have killed a certain number of Mahommedans they are entitled to wear a blue scarf round their waists, and until a man has killed at least one no girl will marry him.

The tribes on the Cabul side of the country wear entire goatskins, but the Bashgol Kafirs, who adjoin Chitral, wear short tunics of woven goats' hair with a broad red binding, on account of which they are often called the "*Siah post*," or black-robed people. The women have a similar tunic fastened across the bosom with a brooch, and with a loop upon the shoulders in which the children are carried. I was fortunate enough to obtain one of these tunics, but could not get a woman's head-dress, to my great regret, as they are very curious and quaint-looking. The men wear nothing on their heads, which are shaved quite bare, with the exception of a little patch of hair on the crown, which is allowed to grow long and to fall down upon the shoulders.

The Kafirs are supposed to be the descendants of the ancient Aryan race who originally inhabited Bajour and Swat and the Peshawur Valley, as well as Kafiristan, but were driven back by Mahommedan invasions from these fertile districts into the inaccessible fastnesses where they now dwell. The puzzling thing is that though the sculptured remains found all over these districts show that the people who lived

The Lowarai Pass, Near Ziakat.

In them were ardent Buddhists, there is no trace of Buddhism to be found in the religion of the Kafirs, which seems to be a pure idolatry, their chief god being Imbra, the creator, and Gish, the War god, whom they propitiate with blood offerings both before and after their forays. It is curious that they use stools, and do not squat down on their heels, as the natives of India do.

Kafiristan, however, is chiefly interesting on account of its position between Chitral, Asmar, and Badakshan, and now that the point of greatest strategic importance has been shifted from Gilgit to Chitral, it is manifestly of vital importance that we should know what sort of a country it is, and whether there are any easy passes into or out of it; for it is quite possible that Kafiristan and not Chitral may eventually be found to be the key of the position. It is said to be quite inaccessible, and it is known that Timur was obliged to leave it unconquered after losing a great number of men in the vain attempt to subdue it.

On the other hand, it is asserted, with some show of reason, that Alexander the Great, starting from Balkh, came down through the western portion of Kafiristan to the Kunar River, near Jellalabad; so it is quite possible there may prove to be a practicable road through it, though the country through which Colonel Holdich and his escort passed was so steep and rugged that it took them seven hours to do a march of eight miles.

The supposed direction of Alexander's march is peculiarly interesting in connection with the recent campaign. It is thought that he sent an advance guard from Jellalabad through the Khyber Pass to Attock, but that he himself with the main body of his troops followed the Kunar River (which was at that time called the Khoes), to Chitral, where he met with a stubborn resistance from a people called the Aspasians, whom he subdued. From Chitral he would seem to have reconnoitred still further up the Chitral River to a place called Nysa, which was about 10,000 feet in height. There he found the country impracticable for troops, and retraced his steps to Chitral.

From the description given of Nysa, and from the similarity of name, it seems very probable that Nysa is the same place as Nisa Gol where Colonel Kelly defeated Mahomed Isa.

From Chitral he proceeded eastwards into Yaghistan, and from there came down the Landai River through the Upper Swat Valley into the present district of Swat, which is probably the country then called "Udyana," "the Park Land."

From Udyana he again turned eastwards, and attacked the rock

183

A GROUP OF KAFIRS

Aornos, which Sir Alexander Cunningham has identified with Ranighat, a ruined city on the top of a rock a few miles across the Indian border, in the territory of the Khuda Kheyls.

Some years ago I was taken up this rock by one of the chiefs of the tribe. It is about a thousand feet in height, and covered with loose boulders of stone, which make the ascent very troublesome and fatiguing. On the top a great many fragments of sculptures were lying about on the surface of the ground—most of them greatly mutilated, for it is laid down in the *Koran* that it is impious to make any graven image, and a true believer will always break one whenever he comes across it.

Most of the figures are representations of Buddha, but I picked up a little statue of an orator, of which this is the photograph, which is of much historical interest.

It is known that after the conquests of Alexander there was a considerable amount of intercourse between Greece and Hindostan. The Hindus seem to have fully appreciated the beauty of Greek art, and Philostratus mentions that they even had statues made by Greek artists or from Greek models. This fragment, damaged as it is, fully bears out this statement, for it is so like as to be almost a copy of the famous statue of Demosthenes at Athens. Demosthenes and Alexander were contemporaries; does it not seem therefore that the man who made this statue in Ranighat must have seen the statue of Demosthenes in Athens, have marched with Alexander across Persia, and have remained behind with others when Alexander went down the Indus?— for we know that Alexander was in the habit of planting colonies in the countries he invaded—or he may have fallen in love with the daughter of the Buddhist priest, and have said like Ruth, "*Thy gods shall be my gods, and thy people my people.*"

The hand was not found at Ranighat. Both it and this sculptured slab were found by Surgeon-Captain Stoney at Takht-i-Bagh near Mardan in 1891. The slab evidently represents a ceremony of initiation—Buddha sitting cross-legged in the middle under a lotus leaf in the usual attitude of contemplation, whilst a priest is pouring oil over the head of the kneeling neophyte. Some of the faces are very Greek in character. It probably formed one of the steps of a shrine. The hand also is interesting. It is holding an alms bowl in which a snake is coiled up, and is the hand of a Buddha, for it is webbed up to the knuckles, and we know from the Buddhistic writings that Buddha's hands were said to be webbed.

GRÆCO-BUDDHISTIC SCULPTURE FOUND
AT RANIGHAT. HAND OF BUDDHA FOUND
AT TAKHT-I-BAGH.

GRÆECO-BUDDHISTIC SCULPTURE FOUND BY SURGEON-
CAPTAIN STONEY AT TAKHT-I-BAGH.

If the Kafirs are the descendants of this ancient Buddhist race—and everything points to the conclusion that they are—it is difficult to understand how they can have so completely lost all traces of their Buddhism.

CHAPTER 22

Arguments For and Against
Retention of Chitral

Whether Chitral is of strategical importance or not in the line of frontier defence is essentially a question for experts, and I will merely state briefly the main arguments for and against its retention.

It is a poor, thinly inhabited country, hemmed in on all sides by precipitous mountains and intersected by narrow valleys. It is quite a small state, its whole area only amounting to 8,800 square miles, the greatest length being 200 miles, from the Khorabort Pass to Asmar. On the north it is bounded by the lofty range of the Hindu Khush, separating it from Wakhan, on the south by the valleys of the Indus, the Panjkora and the Swat Rivers, on the east by Kanjut, Gilgit, Punial, and Dir, and on the west by the mountains of Kafiristan. Its strategical value lies in the fact that there are several fairly easy passes leading from it into Badakshan and Wakhan, both countries which have lately come under the influence of Russia. Of these passes the easiest are the Darkot and Baroghil, the position of which I have already pointed out, and the Dorah, the road from which enters the Chitral Valley only a few miles from Chitral itself.

Sir Neville Chamberlain has put the case for retirement very clearly. In a letter to the *Times*, dated June 6th, he says:

First, as regards the strategical value of the position of Chitral as a means of checking invasion from the north.
The advocates of the retention of this post at any cost base their demand upon the existence of the Baroghil and Dorah Passes, as also upon the circumstance that the Russian frontier line has of late years been geographically advanced to within

twelve miles of the borderland of Chitral. With this statement the argument as regards the facility of access from the north ends—for nothing is said as to the nature of the country that intervenes between the passes and the positions now occupied, or suitable for occupation, by Russian troops, and from which an advancing force must move to reach Chitral. It is, however, accepted as a well-established fact that this dividing distance is a network of barren mountains and small valleys, practically devoid of population or cultivation, and is only to be traversed at certain seasons of the year, consequent upon the rigour of the climate and the absence of forage for animals.

Next, as to the danger which is anticipated should our garrison be withdrawn from Chitral. It is conjectured that a 'diversion' may then be made on that place by a Russian detachment, to be shortly followed by three or four thousand more troops, who will thus be placed in the position of being able to command the three roads leading north, south, and east, by which they may at pleasure have access to either Cashmere, Jelalabad, or Peshawur. My reply to this suggestion is that the forecast is so extremely improbable, if not impracticable, as to call for no serious consideration. A sure and continuous supply of food is a first requisite for the advance of any body of troops. If that provision be not forthcoming the invading force could neither remain in Chitral nor could it advance; and in that case whence are they to obtain this first of necessities? The surrounding valleys could not produce them. It is the want of a sufficiency of food for the inhabitants that tends to drive these people into acts of violence against their neighbours and into going further afield as highway robbers.

The operations now taking place beyond the Peshawur border are the latest evidence of the difficulties attendant upon the feeding of troops employed in such regions. The force under General Low has its base at Peshawur. That place is the terminus of a railway in connection with the whole railway system of India, and the resources of all India as regards transport and supplies are at the disposal of a well-organised military commissariat department. With all these advantages, and after only one occasion of serious resistance on the part of the tribesmen, the advance of General Low's leading brigade was retarded consequent upon an insufficient flow of supplies to the front. Only a wing of infantry could, in the first instance, be pushed forward into Chitral; and this was all that could be done when it was desirable to have made an imposing demonstration on entering that place. Even Colonel Kelly was delayed in leading his gallant band back to Mastuj until arrangements could be made for feeding them.

I may add that the delay to Colonel Kelly's force was caused, not so much by the difficulty of obtaining supplies, for these had all been sent up from Gilgit, but by the trouble of getting transport. The villagers ran away, and it was only after considerable delay and with great difficulty that a sufficient number were collected to carry the baggage and rations; and to enable this to be done the force had to be divided into two parties each of a little over two hundred men.

This question of "*begar*" or forced *porterage* is, indeed, an ever present difficulty both in Gilgit and Chitral. A year's supplies for the troops in the Gilgit agency are sent up during the few summer months in which the passes are open from the commissariat base at Bandipura in the Kashmir Valley Captain Yielding, D.S.O., who is stationed there in charge of the commissariat, having organised a wonderful system of transport. He makes use of the *mirkobans* or native traders, who, now that there is an excellent road all the way to Gilgit, willingly hire out their animals and themselves to carry up the necessary stores. As I came back over the Burzil Pass I met thousands of them making their way up to Bunji, Gilgit, and Chilas. In this way the cruel and oppressive system of forced labour is avoided.

Beyond, the road has not been extended further than Gilgit, and from there the supplies have to be taken on by a corps of hired Balti *coolies*, but when they are insufficient the villagers have to supply men to make up the deficiency. They are, of course, well paid for their work, but they hate having to do it at all. Money, too, is of very little use to them; what they value is food and clothing. What they say is very true: "We can't *eat rupees*, and you take us away from our farms often when we are most wanted, and we shall suffer in consequence from want of food when the winter comes on."

In Gilgit and Kashmir the people have been accustomed for many years to the "*begar*" system under the Kashmir government, and though they do not like it they have grown to accept it as inevitable, but in Chitral they have not, and their dislike to it is so great that I was told they said, "It is better to fight and be killed at once than be carriers of

KASHMIRI VILLAGER.

loads from village to village for all our lives."

If Colonel Kelly experienced such difficulty in moving his little force, when his supplies had all been sent up to him from Gilgit, and all he had to do was to arrange for transport, the difficulties that would beset the Russians may easily be conceived if they ventured across the rugged passes of the Hindu Khush, into a hostile country many miles from their commissariat base, and with the constant danger of being cut off from it, not only by an enemy, but by the far more to be dreaded agencies of nature. They would have no roads such as we have made, and would have to rely upon the foot tracks used by the mountaineers. What they are like may be imagined from a picturesque description given me by a man who had spent some time wandering about amongst these wild passes.

He said: "I was crucified on a ledge of rock, with my hands clasping a projecting point on either side, and a Gurkha holding on to each ankle; and that," he added, "is where the Russian army will have to come across."

It will be remembered that Jemadar Lai Khan's narrative without any intention of striving after effect—merely stating a fact—gives quite as vivid an idea of the nature of these hill tracks. He said, "The road beyond Rushun had been cut. In one place the planks over which the road is carried had been cut away, and a man could only cross with his bare feet; in parts a man with boots could not pass,"

The same view is taken by Sir John Adye,[1] and also by Sir Lepel Griffin, who, in an article in the June number of the *Nineteenth Century*, says very forcibly:

In time of war a small Russian detachment might perhaps occupy Chitral, but the British Empire would not collapse because a few hundred Cossacks foolishly immured themselves in a death-trap, commanded on every side, whence they could only advance to certain destruction, and where, if they remained, the only alternatives would be starvation or surrender. The whole situation is summed up in the consideration that no movement could be made by Russia from the Chitral side unless she were in complete military occupation of Afghanistan or in friendly alliance with the *amir*, because the position of Asmar, just within the Afghan border, absolutely blocks the way.

---

1. *Sitana:* A mountain campaign on the borders of Afghanistan in 1863 by John Adye also published by Leonaur.

Even that inspired madman Skobeleff would have hesitated to advance against English troops in front with a hostile Afghan army on his flank. If Russia were in occupation of Afghanistan, or the Amir were friendly there are many roads over the Hindu Khush far safer and easier than those of Chitral.

Sir James Lyall also is on the same side. One of his arguments is very much to the point. For us to hold Chitral in force when the Russians can only make a feint there, and when their main attack must necessarily be through the comparatively easy passes into Beloochistan is, he says, as though the French were to seize Switzerland, and hold in strength the Alpine passes between it and Germany, when the obvious point of attack is through the plains of Luxembourg.

Since this was written there has been a debate in the House of Commons upon Chitral, and the following extract is taken from the *Times* Report of Sir H. Fowler's speech:—

This was a purely military question, and I, as Secretary of State for India, was incapable of deciding such a question. My colleagues were under the same incapacity, and the present Government must be guided also by military considerations and also by military experts. The House is aware that there is a very considerable difference of opinion upon this question. The House is aware, from publication in the Times newspaper, that Lord Roberts, an authority for whom I entertain very great respect, entertains one opinion; we know from the despatch of the Government of India that the two eminent soldiers who advise that Government—Sir George White and Sir Henry Brackenbury—also agree in that view; and if I understand the view put forward by them, it is that Chitral is of the greatest strategical importance, so far as the heads of the passes of the Hindu Khush are concerned; that the invasion of India from the north-west could be attempted through those passes, and that Chitral, being a weak power, would fall under the power of its strongest neighbour.

But, Sir, the British Government and the Government of India at home have also military advisers. They have as a military adviser, that distinguished field-marshal who commanded the Indian army for a considerable number of years, and who served for upwards of forty years in India, and whom Lord Rosebery described as the highest living Indian military authority—I mean Sir Donald Stewart. As the House knows, there are also Sir Neville Chamberlain, Sir John Adye, Sir Charles Gough, and Lord Chelmsford, all of whom have served in India, and all of whom have served in this district, and these distinguished officers entertain opinions differing from those of Lord Roberts. But the late Government went further, and availed themselves of the best further military advice that they could command. The advice thus given is not part of the State papers which have been published, and it would not be right, therefore, to quote that advice or to give names. But this I may say, that, so far as our military policy was settled, it was guided and settled, so far as military considerations were involved, by and upon the advice of the most eminent military authorities of the day.

I sum up their opinions, so far as the result which they produced upon my mind and upon the minds of my colleagues, to this effect, that the gigantic natural geographical defences of the north-west frontier render the advance of an invading army practically impossible, and that, having regard to these and other considerations, our position is at the present moment practically impregnable; that Chitral is not a place of considerable importance as a base for military reserves, and that it is not useful as a base for military operations, defensive or offensive; that to lock up troops in Chitral or in the Chitral Valley would be an act of the gravest blundering; and that the construction of a military route to Chitral would, in the event of hostilities, be an advantage to an invading force and a disadvantage to a defending force.

The late Government also came to the conclusion that Gilgit was sufficient, as it always has been sufficient, as a point of observation, and that to leave our main line of defence and to establish outposts and form depots of supplies in distant mountain deserts and among these mountain tribes would sadly weaken the strength of our frontier.

These are the main arguments of those who are in favour of the abandonment of Chitral. The principal advocates in this country of the opposite, the "forward policy," have been Lord Roberts and Mr. Curzon. I have nowhere, however, seen so clear a statement of the arguments for retention as in the following passage in Mr. Knight's *Where Three Empires Meet*:

But the valley of Chitral should be as completely under our control, as is that of Gilgit, for it commands some of the lowest and easiest passes across the Hindu Khush, and affords a ready road to India from Bokhara *via* Badakshan. It is known, that the Russian military authorities consider this a favourable route for the invasion of India; it avoids the great natural difficulties presented by the lofty and inhospitable Pamirs, and moreover there is an easy and much-used caravan road running direct from Chitral to Peshawur *via* Bajour.

The town of Chitral itself is situated at the junction of several valleys leading to the very passes which an invader would have to attempt, commanding them all. We should certainly maintain an agency here, as at Gilgit. This has long been meditated, and the late *mehtar* himself repeatedly expressed a wish that a resident British officer should be appointed to his state. The strategical road which will connect India with Gilgit is all but completed. Some authorities are of opinion that this road should be continued up the higher Gilgit valley, through Yasin to Chitral.

Then we should have the key of the Hindu Khush, and what is more, by commanding the lower Chitral valley, be enabled to outflank a Russian army advancing from Herat. Such arrangements might be made with the native states on our frontier as to permit of our constructing still other strategical roads and establishing outposts where, necessary."

And again.

To argue that the natural difficulties presented by these desert mountain regions, render any invasion on a formidable scale from this quarter impracticable, is not to the point. That small bodies of troops can cross the Hindu Khush the Russians have proved, and here a very small body indeed could prove the nucleus of far spreading mischief. If we neglected to keep under our influence the tribes south of the great watershed, these would undoubtedly place themselves on the side of the apparently stronger power. Led by Russian officers, the tribesmen would fight well, and a diversion which we might find very serious would thus be brought about in the event of a war breaking out between the two empires.

How far the defection of our present friends would then extend, it is difficult to foresee. Such an attack could be, no doubt, repelled, provided matters went well with us elsewhere. Our Indian officers are not afraid of the ultimate result; but we should be compelled to send up to this country a considerable force, which we could ill spare, and possibly this is the only object the Russians hope to attain on this part of the frontier.

Now there is little doubt that the above risks can be obviated by the simple expedient of locking the door on our side. A handful of British officers, such as we have at Gilgit, can effect this if the proper steps are taken in time. This particular gate of the Indian Empire is easily held and guarded. It is chiefly a question of inspiring the natives with a confidence in our power to protect them. A firm policy to this end will minimise the chances of a war, into which, however, it is so easy to drift by vacillation.

Since Mr. Knight wrote this the proper steps have been taken, and the handful of British officers have been sent to Chitral, with the result that the Government of India have been obliged to undertake an expedition on a larger scale than any since the Afghan war, and which cannot cost them less than three or four millions, and that too at a time when there is but little money in the Indian Exchequer. As one of the Pathans said, "You *Sahibs* first pave a country with *rupees*, and then you come and walk over it."

After all, whatever the strategical importance of Chitral may be, the question ultimately resolves itself into this: "Can we afford to keep it?" Sir Auckland Colvin says that our constant frontier expeditions are impoverishing the country, and that if we lose India it will not be by Russian conquest, but by our financial inability to retain it; and Sir Lepel Griffin, in the article from which I have before quoted, gives the same warning:

In conclusion I would observe that the policy which has culminated in the costly Chitral expedition is not one that can be justified in the present state of the Indian finances. If we had an overflowing treasury and a large reserve army, a policy of adventure, though unwise, would not be criminal. Military expeditions on a reasonable scale, and to effect quickly a desirable object, are of great advantage in stimulating military spirit, and compelling the troops to shake off the apathy and love of ease which cantonment life must necessarily bring to even the best

196

soldiers. Prolonged peace is good for no army, and a military expedition is far better training than autumn manoeuvres.

But war is a luxury which cannot be afforded by a Government which has been compelled, by financial causes beyond its control, to reduce establishments, increase taxation, and abandon necessary works of public utility and convenience. It is more important to keep India prosperous and contented than to spend enormous sums of money on a policy, the advantage of which is at any rate disputed, and which many hold to be attended with danger and disaster.

The final decision of the Government with regard to Chitral has just been definitely announced. Six companies of the 25th Punjab Infantry with two Maxims are to be stationed in Chitral Fort, the remaining two companies being at Gairat. The 2nd Battalion of the 3rd Gurkhas with two mountain guns is to be at Kila Drosh, the whole of the troops being under the command of Colonel Hutchinson, of the 3rd Gurkhas. The Malakand Pass and the Swat Valley are to be held by a force under the command of Brigadier-General Waterfield—the 15th Sikhs, the 29th, 31st, and 34th Punjab Infantry, with No. 8 Bengal Mountain Battery and a company of sappers.

Three of these regiments will hold the Malakand, and the fourth the bridge over the Swat River. It is calculated that the annual cost of retaining Chitral in this way will be twenty-five *lakhs*, or 2,500,000 *rupees*, which at the present rate of exchange is only about £130,000. The *mehtar* is to be given the assistance of a council of regency until he comes of age; and it is also stated that Sir George Robertson is to proceed at once to Chitral to superintend the settlement of the country. That is in itself a guarantee that the interests of the people will be safely looked after, for, a brave man himself, he has a generous sympathy for a brave though defeated foe. Moreover his perilous journey into Kafiristan, and the influence he acquired over that wild, intractable race, will prove of great service now.

It is well to strengthen our frontier in every way we can, and to give the natives an occasional lesson on the uselessness of resistance; but what really binds them to us, and will bring them to our side, should we ever stand in need of it, is their belief in our justice as well as in our might. Professor Darmesteter translated an Afghan ballad, which shows the existence of this feeling very clearly—

Les çahibs ont la même loi et pour le faible et pour le fort. Grande est leur justice et leur équité. . . . Ils ne font pas dans un procès différence du faible et du fort. L'homme d'honneur ils le traitent avec honneur. Ils ne protègent pas le bandit, le coquin, le joueur: naturellement ils exercent la royauté.

It is this, and our habit of trusting the very men who have fought against us, that attaches these warrior races to us. It is so utterly unlike their own methods, and it appeals to them the more strongly on that account. The recent conduct of the wild tribesmen of Hunza-Nagar has proved this fully. We have already acquired so strong a hold upon the affections of these wild tribesmen that they, who in 1892 were engaged in fighting us, this spring were our loyal and effective allies. When levies had to be raised amongst them, more than eight hundred men volunteered, though only one hundred and fifty could be taken, as there would not have been sufficient rations for the rest upon the march.

The others thereupon volunteered to supply themselves with three weeks' supplies, and to serve either as fighting men or as *coolies*. It is not unlikely that it may prove necessary to subdue the turbulent tribes of Yaghistan before we can fully establish peace on our border; and should there be an expedition against them or another Black Mountain expedition, it may confidently be predicted that the Chitrali levies will be amongst our most efficient troops.

www.ingramcontent.com/pod-product-compliance
Lightning Source LLC
Chambersburg PA
CBHW021056090426
42738CB00006B/372